Find Your
Inner Voice

A 6-Week Program for Unlocking the Body's Intuition

Find Your Inner Voice

Using Instinct
and Intuition Through the
Body-Mind Connection

KAROL WARD

New Page Books
A Division of The Career Press, Inc.
Franklin Lakes, NJ

FIND YOUR INNER VOICE
EDITED AND TYPESET BY KARA REYNOLDS
Cover design by Dutton & Sherman
Printed in the U.S.A. by Book-mart Press

To order this title, please call toll-free 1-800-CAREER-1 (NJ and Canada: 201-848-0310) to order using VISA or MasterCard, or for further information on books from Career Press.

The Career Press, Inc., 3 Tice Road, PO Box 687,
Franklin Lakes, NJ 07417
www.careerpress.com
www.newpagebooks.com

Library of Congress Cataloging-in-Publication Data
Ward, Karol.
　　Find your inner voice : using instinct and intuition through the body-mind connection / by Karol Ward.
　　　　p. cm.
　　Includes index.
　　ISBN 978-1-60163-040-7
　　　　1. Self-actualization (Psychology) 2. Mind and body. 3. Instinct.
　　4. Intuition. I. Title.

BF637.S4W358 2009
　　158.1--dc22

　　　　　　　　　　　　　　　　　　　　　　　　　　　　　2008035822

This book is dedicated to my husband, Michael, the love of my life. Your steady support, love, and humor helped make this book possible.

(((((((((Acknowledgments)))))))))

Many people supported me in the writing of this book, and I want to thank them: Michael Pye and the team at Career Press for giving me this opportunity to have my book published. My agent, Sharon Bowers, and owner Angela Miller from the Miller Agency, who gave me the chance to become an author. To Francine LaSala, who originally got my words and ideas into a coherent form.

Thanks to my husband, Michael Souveroff, whom I cannot imagine life without. You gave me the space to write and allowed me to lean on you. I love you very much.

Thank you to Melissa Rosati for talking and walking me through this process. I so appreciate your insight, warmth, and guidance. To Diane Gallo, whose kindness, support, and wonderful eye helped get my words flowing.

Thank you to my reader panel, Rebecca Kendall, Jeanette Bronee, and Marcus Brooks, for taking the time to read my manuscript and give me such insightful feedback. A very special thank-you to Sylvia Moritz for stepping in toward the end with your much-needed energy and talent for words and images.

To my dear friend Amy Torres, who told me with love and conviction that I could do this. Thank you to Lillian Colon and Bari Hyman, my coffee and dance support team.

To my brothers, Charlie, David, and Patrick Ward, who carry words and creativity in their hearts. To my father, Charles Edward Ward, a natural storyteller whose love of people I share.

Thank you to my mother, Dorothy Ward, who has taught me by example to be curious and persevere—I love you.

To my friend Rochelle Rice—our friendship, daily calls, and deep connection mean the world to me. Thank you for being my cheerleader and shaking the pom-poms when I needed them the most.

To all my clients who had the courage to face their pain, open their hearts, and share their lives with me—thank you for your trust.

(((((((((Contents)))))))))

(((((((((Introduction)))))))))

When I started mulling over the idea of this book, I bumped into stories about instinct and intuition everywhere I went. Everyone I met, it seemed, had an experience or a desire to use those abilities more. Businesspeople, artists, teachers, and lawyers all shared with me how they had used their instincts and intuition. They told me, "Oh yeah, I always use my gut when I do business; never go against it," or "My intuition shows up every time I need it; that tingle on my neck lets me know it's working." I had others ask me, "Intuition and the body? How do I find it?" I ended up having long, enriching conversations about the power of the body and its ability to give us important information. I had numerous discussions with a variety of individuals who longed to tap into the guidance their instinct and intuition could give them. They wanted the kind of information that would help them understand their health issues, relationship choices, career direction, and need for personal growth. Through all my interactions, I kept getting the confirmation that this was something that people believed in and wanted to know more about. The topic seemed to resonate, and after receiving enough instinctive signs and intuitive signals of my own, I decided to forge ahead and write.

This book comes from a lifetime of working with my belief in the power of the body-mind connection. My passion has been to study, understand, and show others how this connection provides us with the information we need, when we need it. When we reestablish the bond we have with our bodies, we create an inner security that will help us when we want or are forced to take on even bigger challenges in life.

It is my strongest conviction that when we disconnect emotionally, psychologically, and spiritually from our bodies, we lose the part of ourselves that knows the truth: that core place, the center of who we are, which helps us navigate through life and provides us with knowledge—our inner voice. I have known people who have spent years searching for their own inner voice, the one that has their best interests at heart. I have also seen so many reclaim their bodies, with all their instinctive and intuitive wisdom, and witnessed their deep transformation.

What does is it feel like to be united in body and mind? To have the innate trust in your ability to make decisions? Empowering. When you know in your heart that your choices come from the part of you that follows your best interests, you know you can rely on yourself. When you have yourself, you have everything you need to venture forth in life. That is why I wrote this book. I wanted to give you all the information I could to help you find your inner voice, the one that knows you so well.

Through reading this book, you will discover through reading this book that your inner voice can guide you through whatever is put in your path. So, use the book as you need to. If there are areas in your life that need particular attention, then go right to those chapters. If not, just follow each week as it is listed. As you explore all or some of the chapters in this book, you will see from the exercises and experiences of others how your body and mind can work together. No longer will you feel the split between your heart and head. Your instinct and intuition will be there to guide you. You will understand that when you trust your body, you have the foundation for living a fuller, happier, and more complete life.

((((((How to Use This Book))))))

This book distills my years of work with individual clients as well as workshop groups. It features carefully structured exercises that will not only help you connect to your instinct and explore your intuition, but also understand the obstacles that keep you from hearing your inner voice. My clients have given me permission to share their personal experiences. I chose to change some of the identifying factors of their stories, but the dilemmas and triumphs they experienced are true. As you work through the book and complete the exercises, you will learn to turn up the volume on what one client calls the "quiet whisper inside."

The book is designed in a 6-week format. Starting with Chapter Two, in each week you will focus on a different area of your life. All the exercises and checklists in this book are called **Compass Points**, and you'll see a small compass icon at each spot. The exercises build upon each other.

Compass Points were designed to help you figure out *your direction* by using *your body* as a guide. You will be asked to explore a variety of different aspects of who you are in order to strengthen your body-mind connection. At the end of each chapter, there are assignments for you to try during the week.

Buy a notebook or journal that you can carry with you in case you want to use one of the exercises to help you solve a problem in that moment. Each time you try an exercise—and you should do each more than once—make a journal entry, and reread your previous entries to see if anything's changed. This is a great way to follow the progress you're making in building an internal network of connections between the body and mind. If you can, picture being lost in a forest and using a compass for the first time and not quite knowing how it works. The more familiar you become with your body compass and the responses it gives you, the more you will trust its messages.

As you reconnect to your own body's unique way of telling you important information, you will know deep down exactly what feels right to you. Your long-suppressed instinct will come back and you will no longer over-think. You'll begin to call on your own inner voice, the one that never lies, to make your decisions. You'll begin to trust your decisions and your ability to evaluate and respond using the full capacity of your native intelligence. By taking this exciting journey of self-discovery, you will find the answers you need to live a fulfilling life. And, ultimately, isn't having trust in yourself what it's all about?

(((((((((Chapter One)))))))))

Your Body's Talking—
Are You Listening?

...As with the migrant birds, so surely with us, there is a voice within if only we would listen to it, that tells us certainly when to go forth into the unknown.

—Elisabeth Kubler-Ross

It was late afternoon, nearly rush hour, and I was on my way to look at an apartment for rent on the Upper West Side of Manhattan. I took the subway to 116th and Broadway and got off on a very long platform. I had two options to get up to the street: I could either take the stairs via the 114th Street exit, or leave by the 116th Street exit. Because I was much closer to the 116th Street exit, I pointed myself in that direction. But as I faced the stairs to leave, I felt a fast current of energy move through my chest, and without thinking, I found myself turning around and heading the longer distance to the other way out.

When I got to the street level, I started to cross the avenue toward my destination. Suddenly, I heard a screech of tires, and watched as a yellow cab jumped the curb at 116th and Broadway. Careening wildly, it plowed right into a crowd of people and skidded into a storefront window, shattering the glass—exactly where I would have been standing had I taken the closer exit. As I stood in shock, I realized the quick quiver of energy I felt on the subway platform helped me avoid a serious accident.

Have there been times when you have made choices without thinking, choices that may have seemed irrational or illogical at the time, but that turned out to be important and life-bettering? You know, that feeling of *knowing without knowing?*

The hunches, gut feelings, and head-, neck-, and heart-pounding sensations that you feel at different moments are your body's way of telling you the truth. These seemingly random and elusive physical signals come to you from the connection between body and mind.

Is it possible to tap into those signals on a more consistent basis? Absolutely. You can learn to use this overlooked pathway of knowledge and information to make all kinds of decisions—ordinary, everyday decisions such as, Should I stop at the bakery on my way to work? Which route should I take to the store? Or larger life decisions that affect your future personal and professional goals, such as, Should I quit or take the new job? Is this person really right for me to date, marry, or live with? By learning to trust your body's signals, you will find yourself more able to consistently decide what brings you happiness and fulfillment.

YOUR INNER VOICE

How do you harness this power? By learning to notice, access, interpret, and apply the information shared through the body-mind connection. Many times we find ourselves in a struggle between our head and our gut: We dismiss physical signals, symptoms, and sensations, and go with the logic of our minds. We try to make choices based on what we think we *should* do as opposed to what really *feels* right for us. And although there is nothing wrong with logic, it can be a one-dimensional way of figuring things out. The key to opening up your intuitive and instinctive awareness is to include your body in the decision-making process. Learning to live "from the inside out" allows your inner voice to emerge.

What is your inner voice? It's that quiet part of you that says *pay attention to me,* there is something here you need to be aware of. Your inner voice includes both *instinct* and *intuition*. These words are often used interchangeably to describe reactions that seem to have very little to do with the mind, but the main difference between instinct and intuition is that your instinct has a biological sensation, a quick, physical flash or a steady nagging, whereas intuition seems to just appear or float into our consciousness.

Because flickers of instinct and intuition occur so quickly and unexpectedly, we often dismiss them. But what if you could understand more of what you were receiving? What if you formed a relationship with your body and learned to understand its language? What if you could learn to translate these apparently random signals of instinct and intuition into a dependable guidance system? You can. It's simple. You can learn to cultivate a strong body-mind connection.

INSTINCT

Instinct is the body's primal method of navigating in the world and encompasses the immediate biological reactions that allow you to make quick decisions. Instinct makes you hit the brakes when a ball rolls into the street, or keeps you from hiring the babysitter with the great references because it just doesn't feel right. Instinct prompted you to go after that new position, even though you weren't quite the right fit—and you ended up getting the job.

Our instincts are part of an internal system of self-care that helps us manage our pleasure, pain, and survival ability. This stream of signals gives us an ongoing set of body reactions and responses that yield an incredible amount of knowledge. The flutter in the chest, tension in the shoulders, tingle up the spine—these are all clues that your body wants to tell you something. The more connected you are to your body, the more your instinct will be available to you in the form of feelings, sensations, and that "knowing without knowing." When you fine-tune your awareness, you'll be able to clearly hear, translate, and facilitate the instinctive conversation between your body and mind. You'll be able to understand and trust more of what your body is saying and apply it in your life.

At the subway station, my instinct told me to take the other exit even though I was much closer to the first one. My body sent me a signal, and I listened without thinking, and chose to go the other way. If I had ignored the current of energy that went through me, my story would have had a less-happy ending. I certainly would have been seriously hurt, or even killed. Perhaps my *intuition* was also at play.

INTUITION

Although instinct and intuition seem to share some traits, they are also slightly different. Whereas instinct often has a basis in a physical sensation, intuition seems to appear out of the blue. However, the more connected you are to your body, the more available you will be to pick up on intuitive flashes. Waking up the body activates and facilitates both instinct and intuition, because all your body circuits are in operation; those intuitive flashes have more of a chance to make themselves known.

It's like when you have the unexpected desire to call a friend you haven't talked to in a long time and she says, "I was just thinking of you!" Intuition happens in those moments when you hear or get information you have no way confirming. My grandmother, who lived with us when I was a child, would sometimes wake up in the morning and insist upon going to play bingo at the American Legion that night. She inevitably would win the grand prize of the night—the biggest jackpot. Later she would tell us she just had this flash that she needed to go play, and that she would probably win.

My clients describe intuitive flashes as the impulse to check on their sleeping children, and finding them ill. They talk of running into people whose names appeared in their consciousness the day before, and felt those seemingly random tingles up the spine right before the phone rang, knowing who it would be.

So although instinct and intuition are slightly different, they both serve to give us knowledge for living happier lives. And using your body as the compass is the key. Once you connect to your body, your instinct and intuitive ability becomes sharper. You pick up on more signals. What

was once muddy and confusing clears up. You form a partnership with your body and align yourself to your inner
voice.

THE SCIENCE OF INSTINCT & INTUITION: A HISTORY OF GUESSWORK

In recent years, there has been a lot of talk about "the
other brain," the one that exists in the gut. In an article entitled "Through Analysis: Gut Reactions Gains Credibility,"
The New York Times interviewed social psychologist Dr. Gerd
Gigerenzer. A researcher in the science of heuristics (a
method of problem-solving based on educated guesses and
intuitive judgments), Dr. G's studies show that our
"hunches" are often more accurate than our most logical
thinking. His work further illustrates that a classical, rational approach is slow and demands too much information.
Dr. Gigerenzer says that when people rely on their gut feelings and use the instinctual rule of thumb to "go with your
first best feeling and ignore everything else," it can permit
them to outperform the most complex calculations.

In another article entitled "Get Out of Your Own Way,"
published in the science section of *The Wall Street Journal*,
reporter Robert Lee Hotz wrote about studies being done
in Germany, Norway, and the United States. He says, "In
ways we are only beginning to understand, the synapses
and neurons in the human nervous system work in concert
to perceive the world around them, to learn from their perceptions, to remember important experiences, to plan ahead,
and to decide and act on incomplete information. In a rudi-
mentary way, they predetermine our choices."

I find these studies fascinating, because whether or not
you trust your inner voice yet, they prove there is a definite

brain-gut connection. This keeps the idea of instinct and intuition grounded in the reality of science, and shows us how that the body and mind do work together. But although I like science, I'm an extremely practical person, and my interest is on a different level. I want to know: how do we get there?

FOUR LITTLE WORDS

Most of our decisions are made by the voice in our heads—our thoughts, or our "reason." But every time we're faced with a decision, our bodies have an opinion too. My goal is to show you how to tap into your body's messages to improve the quality of your life.

This is not to badmouth our brains; we need all the advantages our intellect has to offer. But in today's world, we tend to be mind-heavy. To have a more complete view of the world, we need to bring things more into balance. This means making the mind and body allies.

So what really is the difference between the messages that come from our bodies and the ones that come from our minds? It can be summed up in four little words: *the body doesn't lie.* However, its reactions can certainly be complex. We carry a variety of amazing processing systems within us, each with a specific job. Yet, the more disconnected we are from our bodies, the more we confuse its messages. We might mistake hunger for fatigue, or drink more caffeine to keep going, when what we really need is a nap. We rely on our minds to make our decisions for us, but our minds are forever making rationalizations. Perhaps we stay with a boyfriend or girlfriend because we "think" he or she might change, when, deep down, we have a feeling they won't. Or maybe we convince ourselves to choose a career path picked by others because it's sensible, even though we have other dreams.

Every minute, every day, our bodies give us feedback about our functioning. Our stomach growls, and we know we are hungry. Our ankle swells, and we know we are injured. We yawn and stretch, and we know we are tired. For that reason, we can look to our physical bodies to give us their best first impressions. Besides informing us about our physical states, our bodies clue us in to our emotional and intuitive states. The more we understand and accept ourselves emotionally, the more we can trust what our intuition has to say.

As you begin to explore and become familiar with more of your instinct and intuition, you will inevitably strengthen the part of you that has the answers. Your body's physical sensations will kick in, as they did with Allison, a junior fashion designer for a major design house. Although it wasn't her dream job, Allison was content. Shortly into her second year on the job, though, Allison began to feel uneasy. There was no problem she could pinpoint, but just a nagging feeling in her stomach that all was not right. She wasn't treated differently, and people were pleasant, but she still felt something was wrong. She sat with the feeling for about two weeks, and then decided she was going to speak to her manager about her impressions. I encouraged her to do so. The next day, Allison asked her manager if something was happening at the company, and if her position was in jeopardy. Her manager looked at her in shock and said, "How did you know?" Allison said, "I don't know, but what *should* I know?" Her boss told her that Allison and a few of her colleagues were going to be let go in the next month because of budgetary cuts. Allison later told me she was actually quite calm when she heard the news because on some level she already knew. Allison now owns and operates her own successful fashion company, but she still remembers how her body gave her the heads up.

FEELING MORE ALIVE

When clients work through my exercises to get them back in touch with their bodies and their bodies' *signals*, a magical thing happens. I can actually see the moment they connect to their bodies and the instinctive understanding of what they need to do to improve their lives. Their eyes brighten, their faces open up, and their shoulders relax as their instinct and intuitive awareness starts to flow. I watch bodies transform, becoming more expansive and upright. The heaviness of not knowing how to move forward begins to lift. They look and act more alive, because they *are* more alive. Their willingness to get into their bodies and explore its messages allows them to reconnect to their intuitive self where the answers wait. The answers have always been there, but now they are obvious. I know their journey, because I took it too.

MY JOURNEY

Many times throughout my life I went against what appeared to be the right answer and went more with what I *felt*. I didn't listen to the messages from my mind, because the instinctive sensations in my body told a different story. These choices involved decisions about my career, moving to the big city, and knowing that my husband of now 13 years was the one I was supposed to spend my life with. These kinds of intuitive moments were not new to me. For though I thought and analyzed many of these questions, what ultimately made my decisions for me was how those choices made me *feel*, how opting for one thing or another actually *felt* in my body—the difference between a warm flush of excitement when I thought of moving to New York, and a queasy ripple of nerves when I considered staying at the college I was attending. Those are the sensations to which I paid attention: tightening or tenseness versus physical relaxation. It isn't that one feeling is bad or good; it's that the feelings are clues and mean something. Your body is saying that if it does or doesn't feel good, pay attention.

But, later in my life, I had to relearn to trust my body and what it was telling me. When I was younger, I would often know the outcome of many situations that I couldn't possibly have known about in advance. I would feel a wave of energy come through my body, and then an image or picture of what was to happen would form in my head. When I was 11 years old, our Girl Scout leader randomly pulled names out of a hat to decide who would give a speech at the local high school. I felt the energy expand in my chest, and then a picture of me standing in the high school gym came to mind. A moment later, the troop leader called out my name.

Another time I auditioned for a college musical, and as I joined the crowd of students waiting to read the casting list, the same energy washed over me. In my mind's eye I saw my name on the cast list next to character of the comic lead—a part for which I never tried out. When I finally saw the list, my name was there. Little incidents such as this occurred all the time. When I scooped ice cream at a summer job between semesters, I'd guess what flavor someone would order before they did. Or when I was a waitress during the school year, I'd play the same game when my customers ordered lunch. Although my average was pretty high, I never gave my little games any credence.

After I made the decision to leave the college I was attending, I moved to Manhattan to become a performer. During this time, I lost touch with my instinct and intuition. I wanted to be in the city, but had no idea who I was or where I was going. I studied acting but struggled with my body image and self-esteem, and couldn't always express my feelings. A friend recommended a therapist whose training was in body-mind psychotherapy. This type of therapy, which would eventually become my future profession, focused on the body's ability to manage emotional pain through muscular tension. The more you could release the tightness of the muscles and process what was causing it, the more connected you would be to your emotions.

As I connected to my body more, my ability to sense information came back. I learned to pay attention to the flashes of insight rippling through the pathway between my heart and head. I regained what I had lost, and, in time, I began using my abilities more and more. I wanted to help others, so I started a practice as an intuitive counselor. My goal was to show people how to forge and trust the body-mind link, because I saw that when they did, the answers they needed would appear.

Looking for Answers

Clients often arrived in my office in an anxious state, their minds filled with chatter and questions. Should I stay with this guy? Will I get that new condo? Will my career path be secure? I would ask them to stop talking and reconnect to their body. I would say, "Let's take a few moments to see if we can discover some answers." I would have them slow down, calm down, and just breathe for a few minutes. Then I would ask, "What's your body telling you about this guy, this property, that career?" Sometimes they got a definitive answer; sometimes they knew they had to make a decision but were not ready to. The answers would come as they allowed themselves to include their bodies in the decision-making process.

Working with a variety of clients confirmed for me an important and consistent observation: instinct and intuition are not silent, mysterious processes, but could be elusive. Going with my gut and "listening" for those intuitive sensations was becoming more natural for me, but this wasn't true for everyone. In fact, most people are not in touch with those abilities at all, and what gives them the most trouble is *accessing* them. They are out of touch with the sensations their body is sending them.

At last I saw that my true vocation was to empower my clients to make sense of those random physical signals. I could help them learn how to use their bodies as a *compass*. I could show them how to easily call upon and trust their instinct and intuition using the closest and most tangible resource they possessed: their own bodies.

BODY TALK

When the body wants something, it makes itself perfectly clear: it sends a signal. When it wants food, it produces hunger pains. When it wants sleep, it becomes fatigued. When our instinct and intuition are alive and well, the body produces a signal: tightness in the chest, butterflies in the stomach, a tingling in the back of the neck. But because these sensations don't always seem to correlate with how we make decisions with our heads, we tend to ignore them.

The mind will say, "My boss is a great person, she said she's going to give me a promotion," but meanwhile the stomach feels uneasy or the neck feels tingly. Because those sensations aren't a response to a direct physical threat, the signals sometimes get ignored. Only after we realize that the promotion is not offered do we get confirmation that the body's reaction was accurate.

Our bodies do send us messages, but if we are not open to receiving them, if we are not in touch with our bodies, the messages go unheard. It's like hearing the phone ringing, but not really registering it until it's too late and the other person has hung up. We get distracted by what's right in front of us and miss out on what we really need and desire to hear. That potential, that intuitive and instinctual voice, is wasted. When we rely more on what our scientists refer to as the body's "secret brain power," we will be able to take the steps we want with more confidence. Then our potential for making life-enhancing decisions will be fully realized.

IT'S YOUR BODY, LEARN HOW TO USE IT

So, how can *you* start working with your body? The first thing you need to do is give yourself the time and attention you need to pick up on the signals. Listening to your body is like listening to your car radio: As you move from one area to the next, the radio's ability to pick up different stations goes in and out. Sometimes the radio station signal fades away, and sometimes it gets stronger. Because different frequencies are being broadcasted all the time, you need to turn the dial to pick up on the right station. You often have to use the search feature to assist you in zeroing in on the strongest signal possible. The same goes for tuning in to your body. You use your own internal search feature, *your body compass,* to consciously tune in to and receive instinctive and intuitive information.

In order to do this, you'll need to learn how to use your body like a compass. A compass aligns itself with the Earth's magnetic field and is used to help you find your way. It is round, like a watch, and has a needle that always points north, which allows you to determine where south, east, and west are as well. If you become lost, you will always know where north is, and thereby get your bearings.

BODY COMPASS IMPRESSIONS

"Gut instinct" or "go with your gut" are common ways we talk about instinct and intuition. But we all feel our instincts in different ways and in different places. Some people really do get a feeling in the stomach, others in the chest, and still others on the backs of their necks. Different bodies, different signals. Yet there are some general areas in the body where many people experience similar responses. Here are some clues to help guide you in locating your own instinctive body sensations.

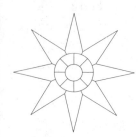

COMPASS POINTS
BODY MAP CHECKLIST

Here are some common sensor spots. Start at the top of your head and travel downward.

- **Eyebrows:** Between the eyebrows and/or above each eyebrow.
- **Neck:** At the base of the neck, middle of the neck, or right where the neck goes into the back of the skull.

- ❀ **Shoulders:** The middle of the shoulders, right where the shoulder blades meet, across the top of the shoulders, and even on the outside of the shoulders.
- ❀ **Chest:** In the middle of the chest, to the right or left of the breastbone, and directly over or next to the heart.
- ❀ **Stomach:** Upper stomach, lower stomach, and on the sides of your torso.
- ❀ **Hands:** Palms, fingertips, and back of the hands.

Of course, there are other places where you will experience physical reactions as well. Many have felt sensations in the feet, the insides of their arms, or at the top of their scalps. Everyone's reaction is unique to them.

THE "FIND YOUR INNER VOICE" JOURNEY

Throughout the years, I've met many clients with great interest in using their instinct and developing their intuition. They attend workshops and read a variety of books, but wind up discouraged because the books take for granted that the reader can feel or picture something within their bodies as easily as the trained intuitive. These readers struggle because although they understand the concepts of instinct and intuition, they can't apply them. They are missing the important first step: *how to connect to the body so that instinct and intuition become second nature.*

In my "Find Your Inner Voice" goals groups, I combine body-mind awareness and goal-setting. Group members create and set individual goals, check in with their bodies to see if they are on the right track, and receive support from other participants. Each gathering begins with a body-mind breathing exercise designed to warm up the body. Then everyone reports on what their body is telling them. I remember so clearly in one of my early groups a member saying to me rather wistfully, "But I can't feel my body." I encouraged her to keep trying the breathing exercise both in- and outside of our weekly sessions, and after the third week she was able to start feeling physical sensations.

Most clients understand the idea of visualization for the body, but do not have the ability to *feel* their bodies. This results in frustration and a desire to give up. It's like seeing your keys through the kitchen window but being locked out of your own house. You can see what you want sitting there on the counter, but you can't get to it. I wanted to help my clients "find their keys" by opening up the door between body and mind, and making the access natural, obvious, and attainable. If I could teach them to sense and hear their inner voices, they could use the guidance to point them in the right direction. Similarly, once *you* know where your north is, your ability to travel south, east, and west will become clear.

You can use this method every day to tap in to your inner voice. If you give yourself the time to pay attention, you will notice results, usually within six weeks. Sometimes it's faster, and sometimes it takes the whole six weeks. Once you become familiar with the exercises, using your instinct and intuition will start to become effortless. I designed these exercises specifically to help my clients unlock and connect to their bodies' instinct and intuitive powers. I wanted to help them get their minds and bodies in alignment so that they could hear and draw upon the knowledge inside. When you connect to your body's wisdom, you unlock your potential for transformation.

YOUR TURN

Before you do any of the exercises, *read each one through once or twice.* Then really focus on what each concept means to you, and describe what the actual *physical* response feels like. Exactly *where* in your body do you experience each one—and exactly *what* do you feel? What is the nature, quality, or intensity of the sensations you perceive? You will be surprised at how descriptive your words will be. For our first exercise, open your journal or notebook and date the page. Take a moment to review the **Body Map Checklist** in this chapter, so that you can have a general body roadmap.

The following exercise will help you identify and link physical sensations to your emotional responses.

COMPASS POINTS

Exercise: Good Feelings/Bad Feelings

1. Close your eyes and imagine something or someone who makes you **happy**. Maybe it's your spouse or your child? Your pet? A beautiful sunset on a Caribbean island?

2. Notice in your body where you feel that feeling of happiness. Put your attention on that area for a few moments. Slowly open your eyes.

3. Write down where in your body you experienced the happiness image. Was it in your hands, chest,

stomach, or toes? Be as specific as possible about the location of the feeling.

4. Now describe in words the feeling you got in your body. What is it exactly? Is it a flush of excitement, butterflies in your stomach, heat in the chest, tingling in the hands, or a melting feeling in your muscles?

5. Now close your eyes again and imagine something or someone who makes you **unhappy**. Is it your boss? A food you don't like? A person who has wronged you in some way? A color you don't like?

6. Write in your journal where in your body you are experiencing the unhappiness the image brings you. Is it in your hands, chest, stomach, or toes? Be as specific as possible about the location of the feeling.

7. Describe the feeling. What is it exactly? Is there tightness, pain, a feeling of nausea? Do your shoulders ache or feel tense?

8. Now close your eyes and imagine something or someone that makes you feel **calm and peaceful**. Is it a serene lake, a beautiful skyline, or spiritual experience?

9. Open your eyes and write in your journal where in your body you are experiencing the calm and peacefulness your visualization brings you. Is it in your hands, your heart area, or your abdomen? Again, be as specific as possible about the location of the feeling.

10. Now describe the feeling in words. What is it exactly? Is it a tingling sensation, a flow of heat, or a sense of total relaxation?

11. Close your eyes again and imagine something or someone that makes you feel **anxious**. Is it a deadline? Paying bills? Visiting with your in-laws?

12. Open your eyes and write down in your journal where in your body you are feeling that anxiousness that the image you are visualizing brings you. Is it in your stomach, shoulders, eyebrows, or forehead? Be as specific as possible about the location of the feeling.

13. Now describe the feeling. What is it exactly? Is it a steel band, a burning sensation, or a fluttery ripple?

14. Take one more deep breath and go back to the image that makes you feel calm and peaceful. Just bring it to mind and let your body respond. Take a few slow, deep breaths, inhaling and exhaling. Open your eyes.

Each time you do this exercise you are building the link between what you feel and its location in your body. Take a look at your answers. Notice the word or words you used to describe the sensations in your body. Were you able to feel things and name them? If you had more trouble feeling things in your body, create the time to do this exercise often. Continue to reinforce this exercise periodically when you are doing day-to-day activities. When you are washing dishes or waiting for an elevator, remember the beautiful images that made you feel happy, and notice where you feel that joy in your body. Then quickly bring up the image of the thing or person that made you unhappy, and notice the feeling. Then quickly switch it back to the happy image. By asking your body to respond automatically while you are doing other things, you are training yourself to feel without necessarily concentrating. This is often when we get unexpected intuitive information. In time, you will start to feel more sensations in your body that are associated with the images you picture. By practicing daily, you will strengthen your ability to sense and feel those signals from your body.

PART I:
The 6-Week Program

(((((((((Chapter Two))))))))))

Week One:
Body Blocks—
Why You Don't Listen

The intuitive mind is a sacred gift; the rational mind is a faithful servant. We have created a society that honors the servant and has forgotten the gift.

—Albert Einstein

A few years ago, I had another Manhattan moment that showed me how our bodies can be our friends—or even our enemies—if we don't listen. I was riding in a taxi on a rainy Tuesday night after a long day at my office. The cabdriver, a big, friendly guy with a strong New York accent, and I got to talking. When he found out I was a therapist, he said, "You shoulda seen the guy I had in here yesterday. He coulda used a therapist." I asked him what he meant, and he said, "I pick up this guy, and I'm taking him uptown when all of a sudden, he starts to hyperventilate. You know, those real fast jerky breaths, in and out and in and out. I'm watching him in my rearview mirror and says to him, 'Buddy, I'm dropping you at the nearest emergency room 'cause you don't look so good.' And the guy says to me, 'Don't bother, there's nothing they can do for me. Just give me a minute.'"

The driver then says, "So I keep driving but I got my eye on him the whole time. After a while he kinda calmed down. He tells me he's been to the emergency room lots of times 'cause he can't catch his breath and thinks he's having a heart attack. But they all tell him the same thing. That there's nothing wrong with him, and he's having some sorta stress reaction. And then he tells me, 'They're right, I'm overloaded. I work 60 hours a week and I'm going through a divorce. I know I should slow down, but I just can't.'" Over his shoulder, the cab driver said to me, "Guess he's too scared to stop moving, so his body's gonna do it for him."

"His body's gonna do it for him." Those words and that story stayed with me a long time. I thought it was sad and poignant that this harried businessman's body was telling him to slow down, but he was too scared to listen. Every instinct he had was yelling that his schedule and circumstances were overwhelming him. But he couldn't or *wouldn't* stop to see what life would be like at a different speed. He chose to ignore his inner voice, even though the volume was up pretty loud.

MIND VS. BODY

With every decision you have to make, two messages usually come from within for you to process: the ones that come from your mind, telling you the logical course of action (as if you were an accountant and life and its experiences were a series of numbers that needed to be balanced on a spreadsheet), and the messages from your body, in the form of a symptoms or sensations. Unlike the mind's message, delivered in "thoughts," the body gives us either a feeling of discomfort, like muscle tightness or pain (in extreme cases, actual illness), or pleasant sensations, like tingling, fluttering, a sense of warmth in the chest, or a flush of excitement that runs from the toes to the head.

Countless times my clients and workshop participants have said to me, "I knew it. I knew I shouldn't have made the choice I did because it didn't *feel* right. But I did it anyway. I talked myself into it." Almost without fail, when I've asked what they meant by "didn't feel right" and had them explore it, they could pinpoint a sensation in their bodies, a physical clue that something was wrong.

However obvious they may be, we don't always listen to our body signals, because we've been conditioned not to. We tend to be rational and are taught from an early age to "use our heads," "analyze the facts," and "think things through." We talk ourselves out of trusting our "gut" because it doesn't always jibe with what's in our heads. When our body tells us one thing and our mind another, we can feel stuck or paralyzed when it comes to making a decision. But nine times out of 10, we fall back on that familiar, logical mind. Yet, from what others share with me, nine times out of 10, going with the mind ends up being a big mistake.

TRUSTING A DIFFERENT SOURCE

No matter how educated or "book smart" you are, anyone who's enjoyed success knows that body perception is a powerful decision-making tool. The signals that come from our bodies are actually a complex set of impulses that time and again prove to be accurate. As mentioned in the previous chapter, I think of those physical signals as points on a compass, which, if attended, can help us make the right choice. When we are in alignment with our five senses and they are flowing, we can use our bodies like a compass and feel beyond what the mind may be advising.

Many people—and I certainly was one of them—don't always value their body signals or rely on them consistently. One reason is because we are bombarded with tremendous amounts of stimuli from the outside world. Technology attracts our attention, whether we want it to our not, either through computers or our ever-present cell phones. These devices are important for our careers, education, and the managing of our schedules, but they can drive our awareness far away from our inner voice.

Another reason we lose touch with our body knowledge is due to the sheer busy-ness of our lives. We move at a fast pace, juggling family, jobs, and friendships along with other responsibilities. It's easy to become overloaded, and we can find ourselves in a state of chronic stress. Similar to our businessman in the cab, being physically hyped-up ends up feeling like the norm instead of the other way around. We don't always end up with the time we need to slow down and connect to our bodies.

The relationship—or lack thereof—we have with our bodies is one of the most important factors in why we miss instinctive and intuitive signals. Sure, we think we have a good bond with our bodies: we're forever looking for ways to care for the physical shells that house our souls; we exercise and carry our bodies to the gym; we eat the all the right foods to keep healthy and functioning; we keep ourselves well-dressed, well-groomed, and well-manicured. But we stop there. We don't really *listen* to our bodies. That's not to say we ignore the signals altogether. When we're hungry, we eat; when we're sick or injured, we see a doctor or health practitioner. But we tend not to hear the messages about things that are more than just the physical.

Most people aren't aware that they are ignoring the sensations from their bodies. It's more like those radio signals I described in the opening chapter; the frequency is not being picked up. More times than not, the signals aren't noticed until after the fact or when an area of our life gets into crisis. So here we are, a group of deeply feeling, emotionally rich human beings who are out of touch with the best instinctive system there is. Whether we pay attention or not, the system continues to operate.

BODY INHIBITION

What is it that creates this disconnection with our instinct and intuition? What causes us to go off course from the life we want to live? There are actually several reasons, and they show up as emotional barriers or body blocks. They are obstacles created by past experiences that we assimilate. They can also be caused by people and situations in our everyday lives that zap our positive energy. These difficulties could be the result of bad self-esteem, or attitudes and behaviors we've been forced to adopt. Whatever the reason, we learn in time to shun our deepest feelings and end up rationalizing our responses more often than not.

Avoiding our emotions takes energy, and we find ways to do so by distracting ourselves. This may take the form of destructive behaviors such as overeating, excessive drinking, or, as in the taxicab story, overworking. Whatever has created these barriers makes it hard for us to access our inner voice. Unless we start to recognize that the blocks

exist, and find ways to understand them, we will feel sepa-
rated from our authentic selves. The good news is that once
we realize those blocks were formed by messages and beliefs that we absorbed, we can start to untangle *who we
really are* from *what we've learned.*

HOW INSTINCT AND INTUITION GET SHUT DOWN

In life, we respond emotionally to people and experiences all the time. We laugh, we cry, we get angry, and we
experience pleasure. In healthy human expression, our emotions have an arc to them; we react, and feelings build and
then are released. I like to describe how we feel emotions by
having you imagine the first big hill on a roller coaster.
Whether you've been on one or not, you can picture how
that initial steep incline is the biggest on the ride. Visualize
yourself going up that first hill and imagine the feelings of
excitement and fear starting to build. Those emotions get
more intense as you move toward the highest part of the
hill. Then you reach the top, and *whoosh*, start speeding down
the other side, screaming your head off! At the bottom, if
the ride were to end there, the coaster would slow down
and come to a stop.

The roller-coaster ride can be used to mirror how we
feel and express feelings. Our emotions travel up a curve
and then down the other side. We respond emotionally, the
feelings start to build; we release those feelings, and then,
just like the end of the roller-coaster ride, we eventually
move into a more relaxed state. Of course, emotional reactions happen at different speeds and vary in length, but the
healthy release of emotions basically follows the same path.

What happens if those feelings don't get released, and for whatever reason are held back? Well, just like the taxi driver's passenger, they don't disappear—we just find ways to keep them at bay, and use our bodies to help us.

THE EMOTION FACTOR

When feelings are not expressed, a physiological adjustment occurs in the body, a protection we create to shut down emotions that might make us uncomfortable. We do this through a physical shifting on the inside and outside of our bodies. We might hold our breath, lock the backs of our knees, tighten our shoulders, or clamp down on our jaws to keep from expressing what we feel. We grip and tighten our muscles so that we don't experience our emotional pain or joy. Wilhelm Reich, MD, who is widely considered to be the father of body psychotherapy, called this *armoring*, the fending-off of uncomfortable or forbidden emotions through physical tension in the muscles. In time the holding-in of our muscles becomes so much a part of us that we don't even know we are tense. We don't sense that our shoulders are up around our ears or that we are clenching our jaws. We often aren't aware until these actions show up as physical pain. When the body starts shouting, that's when we know something is wrong.

Whatever those uncomfortable emotions are, they are unique to each of us. Maybe you were told that good girls don't get angry and boys don't express sadness, or maybe the environment you grew up in did not allow for a lot of emotional expression. You also may be in a relationship or job that is stressful and unsatisfying. Maybe you carry heavy burdens in your life, such as an ill parent or child, and you feel you have to keep it together. No matter what the reason, if you don't allow yourself to feel what you need to, the feelings don't go away. We just find ways to physically manage them and use our bodies to house them. Then we disconnect from our bodies to seal the deal.

That's how Linda, a former client of mine, described her own split from her body. As she started to explore how and where she felt things physically, she also noticed where she *didn't* feel things. She told me, "My body feels numb from the neck down, but my head feels like I'm floating above my body, without being connected to the rest of me." She had discovered a way to cope with painful feelings by disconnecting from her body.

Similar to Linda, many people view their bodies as existing separately from their minds, which can be an obstacle for achieving happiness in life. When we disconnect from the rich emotional expression we have within us, we separate from our instinct and intuition. When that bond is broken, we become restless and dissatisfied. We live our lives with an emptiness inside. We search for fulfillment in short-lived ways and run from the feelings and signals that could guide us toward deeper satisfaction. I've had individuals describe their lives as gray or shallow. They are in unhealthy relationships and boring jobs, and have a lack of purpose. They feel this way because they are out of touch with the inner confidence and guidance they need to make changes.

The more connected we are to our bodies, the more we can pick up on the information it is sending us. The first step it is to become aware that your body is even sending you message. The next important step is to take those signals, listen to what they're saying, and follow the call. And that is how you can connect to your instinct and ultimately to your intuition. A sound body-mind connection will create more balance and flow, and fulfill the eternal longing for a more spiritually satisfying existence. And through writing, visualization, and sensory exercises, you can reclaim your body and turn up the volume on your own quiet inner voice.

WHERE YOU START/WHERE YOU FINISH

My friend Roberta Brenner, who is a life coach, said to me that the first consultation she has with clients often turns out to be a surprise for both of them. What the client thought he wanted to work on when he scheduled the appointment starts to change as he really takes the time to focus on himself. Her clients may think they want to work on their careers, but with exploration end up choosing their physical heath as the priority.

I have found this to be true as well. What you thought you wanted to work on as a goal may change to something else as you listen to your body's wisdom. When you look in the direction your compass is telling you to, you may find yourself on a different path. That's the beauty of using your inner voice. You find out what really matters to you, because your heart and head are working as one. That bond creates an authentic opinion you can trust.

When you include who you are, how you feel, and what you need as part of the goal-setting process, you allow for the possibility of achievement. You cannot make an intention or goal without including your humanness and an understanding of what is going on in your life. That humanity, if honored, is what keeps us in touch with our capacity for change, and informs of what we need to do in order to take the next step.

THE PROCESS OF CHANGE

Change will happen when you start connecting to your instinct and intuition. It's similar to the book I saw one night when I was riding the subway. (I know it seems as though all my lessons and insights about transformation seem to happen when I travel around the city, but I've found, like Dorothy in the *Wizard of Oz*, you can learn a lot in your own backyard.) I was on my way home and glanced over at the woman sitting next to me on the train. She was reading something called *How to Stretch*. From the pictures in the book, I saw it was some kind of manual on how to stretch the muscles in the human body. As she flipped through the pages, with me peering over her shoulder, I could see that each page showed someone bending and reaching in a variety of poses. Glancing at the pictures, I saw that there were many ways to stretch the muscles in our bodies depending on what area you wanted to work on. I continued looking at the poses and started thinking, wouldn't the principles used to stretch our muscles be similar to expanding ourselves to change on a personal level?

I thought about the changes I had made with my own body and how I achieved them throughout the years. During that time, I had been taught some basic principles of stretching. Those principles are:

1. Warm up the body through some kind of easy movement.

2. After your body feels warm, slowly start to stretch your muscles while paying attention to any sign of discomfort.

3. Challenge yourself in time to reach beyond your normal range of movement, and be

prepared for some discomfort as you learn
new movements and postures.

Each of these steps seemed to correspond to what I have witnessed when people go through a process of change. What follows are the ways in which we can learn to stretch and handle new experiences.

Noticing

The guidelines used for stretching are similar to the ones we use when we undergo emotional, psychological, and spiritual transformation. At first, we need to warm up to the idea that change is happening or needs to happen. This may be that quiet voice inside that starts to get louder as it questions the state of your life. You might start to feel restless, anxious, or impatient with how things seem to be the same. You begin to sense what doesn't feel right or notice how routines and activities that used to fulfill you no longer do. Slowly, you are warming up to the idea of change.

Exploring

The second thing that occurs is exploration. Now that you realize things need to shift, you begin to investigate *what* needs to be different. As you start to explore the different aspects of your life that are dissatisfying, a process of self-examination will occur. This might include talking with your husband, wife, or friends about your need for change. You may look to advance your education, check out job opportunities, or examine the need for new relationships. When you start to take steps toward these different areas, you will probably feel a level of discomfort. This happens because you are trying new things and are "exercising" different parts of your personality. You feel the unfamiliar as you try for a deeper stretch in your life.

As you reach toward new ventures, you may feel frustrated, impatient, fearful, and unsure about the success of your new efforts. These are common ways to feel, and are perfectly normal. This brings to mind Karen, a dynamic businesswoman, whose least favorite word was *process*. Whenever she would hit a point of challenge in her personal change journey, she would roll her eyes and say humorously, "I guess I'm just in the *process* of change." I would answer, "Yes, you are. It's a real pain, isn't it?" We would then laugh together because affirming her reality that new beginnings aren't always easy or fun was important. When you validate your right to struggle, because you are growing, it allows you to keep moving toward new experiences. Try not to judge your progression and categorize what's happening as either good or bad. In reality, it's *all* part of your personal expansion.

Changing

In time, you move out of your comfort zone. You notice that your behavior and interests have shifted, and that new choices are now in motion. Although there may be times of intermittent fear or insecurity, you realize that you are experiencing life differently. You have expanded beyond your old normal range of living. Once that happens, you have fully stretched...until it's time to do it again.

We need to apply the same type of care we use for stretching our muscles as we do when we stretch our souls. Respect your need to warm up to the idea. Accept that it will feel uncomfortable at times. Challenge yourself to move beyond what is familiar. After all, once you realize that things need to change, the process has usually already started.

"FIND YOUR INNER VOICE" GOAL-SETTING

As you read this book and decide which areas of your life you want to focus on, you need to take into account where you are personally. Consider who you are as a person and what is happening in your present life. When you create new goals, it's important to look closely at some key life factors and understand how those circumstances will affect your choices. Because we are all different, a one-size-fits-all approach does not work for personal goal-setting. In order to keep your objectives realistic and moving forward, take a look at the current realities of your life.

Often goals are created with the best of intentions, but, in hindsight, leave out some important elements of your day-to-day life. All aspects of family, work, relationships, and responsibilities need to be examined. If you don't include crucial details, you may lose momentum after you craft your goals. For example, Melissa wanted to start running again after the birth of her daughter. She used to run regularly and felt it was the best way for her to get back in shape. Her plan was that she would go back to her old program of running early in the morning, five days a week. Only now she would add in the pushing of a baby jogger. Melissa was excited about getting started and looked forward to getting her pre-baby body back.

When we talked about the reality of her life and I had her check in with her body's reaction to her goal, the response was different. She reported that she felt nervous and physically tense in her shoulders when she sat with the plan. She was worried about her ability to keep up her running schedule because of the lack of sleep and fatigue she felt from caring for her new baby. We used Melissa's body as a compass, asking it, step by step, what she really could do to move toward her fitness goal in a much more realistic manner. We started out with the original number of days she wanted to run, and kept lowering the number until she felt a sense of calmness and relief in her body. She finally decided that she would start on the weekends, first trying one day with the baby jogger and one day on her own. This decision all came from Melissa focusing on her body and the reality of her life. She was able to shape a more realistic goal by paying attention to her body's reaction.

In addition to being realistic, you need to know what you want to work on, your personality style, and how to keep track of your progress. Remember the compass I described in the first chapter and how it aligns itself with the Earth's magnetic north pole? Well, the next two exercises will help you get in touch with your inner compass so that you are aligned with your true self. They are the cornerstone of all the **Compass Points** exercises. If done consistently, they will give a place to find answers.

The Starting Point

One of the best ways to clear the channels of communication between you and your body is through breath work. Simple breathing exercises can be done anywhere, and they are very effective. Their purpose, in addition to getting oxygen flowing nicely to your brain, is to compel you take a timeout; they help create enough distance between your inner world and the world around you. This distance aids your perspective, which can help you make better decisions. You will also find other breathing exercises later in the book that will either calm you down or energize you. This first breathing exercise is the one I use in all my workshops, and is the starting point for body-mind connection.

COMPASS POINTS
Exercise: Four-Part Breathing

(Remember to read through this exercise once before you start.)

1. Close your eyes.
2. Inhale deeply through your nose.
3. As you exhale, imagine the air going up and out through the top of your head.
4. Now, as you inhale, picture the air coming down into and through the top of your head.
5. Exhale slowly through your mouth.
6. Do the same pattern again 5 times:
   - ❀ Breathe in through the nose.
   - ❀ Exhale through the top of the head.
   - ❀ Inhale through the top of the head.
   - ❀ Exhale through the nose. Slowly open your eyes.

Take notice of your body and your energy after you do this exercise. See if you feel more relaxed or calm after you have connected to your breath.

Body Sense

In the next exercise, I have you ask yourself the question, what does my body need? This is not just what the body needs physically, but what you may need overall. I'm not excluding the mind's opinion; I'm just allowing the body to have more of a say than it usually does. The "what does my body need?" question invites the mind's input but has you focus on the information the body has to offer. You will explore these areas: physical, emotional, spiritual, intellectual, and psychological

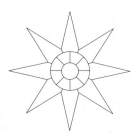

COMPASS POINTS
EXERCISE: WHAT DOES MY BODY NEED?

1. Do the **Four-Part Breathing** exercise.
2. With your eyes closed, ask yourself, "What does my body need?"

   ❈ **Is it physical?** Do I need more rest or relaxation? Do I need exercise? If so, how does my body really want to move? Do I need physical touch such as a massage, a facial, or energy healing? Do I need physical connection with someone in the form of a hug, holding hands, or leaning on someone's shoulder?

   ❈ **Is it emotional?** Do I need an emotional release, such as laughter, crying, or expressing hurt or anger? Do I need to assert myself at work or in my personal relationships? Do I need to express emotion directly to someone, or do I want to release feelings by watching a movie, listening to music, or going for a walk?

❀ **Is it spiritual?** Do I need quiet time, meditation, prayer, conversations about spiritual beliefs, or to go on a spiritual retreat? Is there a larger spiritual picture for which I need answers, and is there a place or person from whom I can get those answers?

❀ **Is it intellectual?** Am I looking for more education, either formally or by learning a new skill? Is it through meeting new people, studying a new language, or learning about politics, medicine, religion, or business? What areas, such as career, money, self-care, or health do I need to stimulate?

❀ **Is it psychological?** Are old habits and patterns holding me back? What do I need to know about myself and my way of being in the world? Is there something I need to understand or change? Do I need to create better relationships and partnerships, work on family dynamics, or understand fears that are holding me back?

As you start asking the question "what does my body need," you will receive information. How it shows up will be unique to each of you. Some people get very vivid images; others get words or see colors—it's all individual. Try not to censor yourself, and when you have gotten information, open your eyes and write it down. Don't worry if you don't get anything right away; you have time to practice during the week.

Remember, the questions in each category are only sug-
gestions. You may get a wealth of information as soon as
you focus on one of the areas. Ask yourself if any of it
matches the goals you thought you wanted to achieve. This
can be a surprising answer, because sometimes we set goals
for things we *think* we want, as opposed to what our inner
voice is telling us it needs.

STAYING ON COURSE

No matter how small your steps, keeping aware of them
will be a good reminder of your progress. Let's look at five
key strategies for you to focus on when you create and set
your goals in motion.

Honor Your Personality

When you are planning goals, it's good to understand
your personality and think of ways to support it. Are you
someone who prefers to do things on your own, or following a book or online course? Do you like to be part of a
group, a classroom, or an association? Are you introverted
or extroverted? Are you a night owl, coming alive in the
evening, or are you a lark, wide awake and energized in the
morning? These are the details that can guide you when
you are creating your goals.

If circumstances have you at odds with your natural
style, it's important to know what you will need to do. Get
more of sense of what works for you by answering the
following questions.

COMPASS POINTS
PERSONALITY STYLE CHECKLIST

* What is your personality style? For example, do you like to approach your goals in a step-by-step manner, or are you someone who likes to focus on the big picture and work toward that?

* Do you approach goals better by yourself, one-on-one, or with a group?

* Are you a morning, afternoon, or evening person?

* If you have to do something that goes against your nature in order to achieve a goal, such as taking a class in the evening when you are a morning person, how can you support yourself with what you need when you are challenged? For example, can you plan to rest before that class, or the next day?

* Remember the times you have been successful in the past. Picture what contributed to those accomplishments and remind yourself of what you put in place to achieve your goals. Write down the successes and what got you there.

Honor Your Circumstances

Be *optimistic* and *realistic* when you create your goals, and pay attention to what is going on in your life. When you look at these factors and modify your timeframe or steps as needed, you will be more satisfied with your progress. You are where you are in life, and sometimes the things you have to adjust for are pleasant, and sometimes there is unexpected heartbreak. Take a look at the following checklist to see if there is anything to which you need to pay attention.

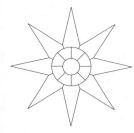

COMPASS POINTS

Life Circumstances Checklist

❀   What is happening right now in your life that requires your attention? Similar to my client with the new baby, are there factors in your life that are new or perhaps not changing for a while?

❀   Taking on new goals and moving toward them means being realistic about certain areas. Write down your compass directions for the following aspects of your life.

    N = not great, **S** = so-so, **E** = eventually, **W** = well.

    ❀   Health:

    ❀   State of Mind:

    ❀   Finances:

    ❀   Family responsibilities:

❀   If any of these are not a **W**, you will need to keep that in mind when creating your goals.

Anchor Your Goals

When you are creating your intentions, anchor them in the pleasure of what you are trying to accomplish. Some goals bring an immediate sense of achievement, but others take time and will bring delayed gratification. Getting a degree in school, finishing a book, working on a relationship, or losing weight are examples of delayed gratification. To build a sense of personal respect, you need to remind yourself along the way that both the goal and you are worth the energy you are expending. Vocal or written statements that honor your effort and acknowledge your steps will nourish your spirit and keep you going. Try a few from the following checklist.

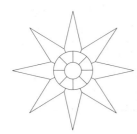

COMPASS POINTS
GOAL ANCHORING CHECKLIST

❋ Write one sentence that reflects and acknowledges the fact that you have decided to move toward what you want. For example: "I acknowledge the fact that even though I don't yet see the results of my goal, I am willing to try." Or, "Even though I have not reached my goal, I am proud of the effort I am putting in, and here is a list of small achievements I have made."

❋ Think of something you are working toward right now that you could put into an acknowledgement statement. Write it down.

Validate Your Achievements

This strategy is often overlooked, yet is vital to achieving what you want. I often make my clients do validation homework. This means they have to come in with a written list of all the accomplishments, no matter how small, they achieved during the week. You would not believe the resistance and skepticism I have run into when I assign this. Yet, each time this assignment was completed and reviewed, the person doing it would feel her energy shift. She would tell me she felt lighter, upbeat, and relieved. I had her read her accomplishments out loud, and pause after each item to receive congratulations from me. I did this so that she could really take in what she had achieved.

This is a great exercise to do with a friend, loved one, or anyone you trust. You can also do it on your own by stating your accomplishments out loud and then saying something to yourself similar to "good job" or "that was a great effort"—anything that makes you feel good.

Here are some questions for you to answer about your style of validation.

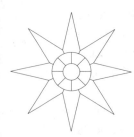

COMPASS POINTS

ACHIEVEMENT VALIDATION CHECKLIST

How would you like to acknowledge your achievements along the way?

- **Visually:** Checkmarks or stars on a calendar, flowers at the end of the week, a sign on your door that says "Good Job"? What works for you?

- ❀ **Verbally:** With whom do you want to check in and share your daily, weekly, or monthly accomplishments? Is it a friend, teacher, relative, therapist, coach, or online community?
- ❀ **Tangibly:** Is there a present or service with which you can reward yourself? Massage, dinner, a theater ticket?

Evaluate Your Efforts

Evaluating how effective your efforts are will keep you from giving up when you hit stumbling points. In addition to the previous strategies, knowing what needs to be modified will keep things flowing. Sometimes people give up rather than fine-tune some part of their goal that is not working. This could mean you have to slow down, take smaller steps, or bring in support. Once you have made those adjustments you can keep going. Just say to yourself, "I'm picking up where I left off," rather than "I'm starting over." This way, all the experiences you had before you hit that stumbling point will still count. You are simply picking something back up that was put down for a moment and reminding yourself that, despite the snag, you are continuing forward. That in itself is an accomplishment.

BECOMING STUCK

What happens if we do get stuck along the way? We all know the feeling. We have a goal in mind and yet can't seem to move toward it and take the action we need to. We sit with the task, question our feelings, avoid talking about it, and wonder what's keeping us from moving forward. It's frustrating, brings up feelings of inadequacy, and raises two questions: Why do we get stuck? And how do we unstick ourselves?

Why We Get Stuck

There are many individual reasons for becoming stuck, or what I call *pausing*. Throughout the years, clients have described their stuck-ness to me in the harshest of terms. They say they're stuck because they are lazy, stupid, resistant, and lack willpower—not the most motivating statements for getting unstuck. In my experience, there are three main reasons why people get stuck. They are fear, the need for reassurance, and the need for information.

Fear

Throughout this book, you will read stories about people who wanted change in their lives. You will see how their process sometimes started with the fear of taking action, but fear also crops up after the journey has started, and that's when you can find yourself stuck. Understanding what it is you are afraid of, and why it has shown up now, is important. Rather than making your fear the enemy, you need to make it more of an ally. You have a fear response for a reason, and you need to understand whether it is based in reality or not. Either way, using your fear as a clue, not a club, will help you discover what you need to do to move through it.

Reassurance

We all need reassurance when we decide to try new things. Whether you are a CEO or going back to school for the first time in 20 years, you need good people to advise you. It makes me think of how young children discover the world. At around the age of 2 or 3, children start to actively explore everything around them. If you watch them, you will see how they take a few steps, look back at their mothers, take a few more steps, and look back again. They use that relationship for security and encouragement. And even though you aren't 2 years old, you will still need reassurance every once in a while. So when you find yourself feeling stuck, ask yourself who could provide you with some solid support.

Information

If you find yourself unable to take action, but it feels more frustrating than fearful, you are in need of information. That could range from the general to the specific. You want to start a fitness program but are confused by the choices, so your plan stalls. You want to buy a house but because you don't understand how to get a mortgage, you don't take the steps. You need solid information and have to actively seek it.

This is where your body's wisdom will come in handy. As you learn to connect to your inner voice, through the strategies in this book, you will get a clearer picture of what you need. When you understand and resolve your fear, get reassurance, or receive information, you become unstuck.

A FINAL THOUGHT

Although I don't believe that berating yourself is motivational, I do understand that having consequences, especially painful ones, can be useful. I make this distinction, because not all the actions we take to unstick ourselves come from a place of understanding and compassion. Sometimes we have to have the experience of an uncomfortable consequence, such as getting a poor performance review or a bad grade, in order to shift our behavior.

But there is a difference between *consequences* and *criticism*. Learning from the consequence takes you further than berating yourself for it.

Use the following exercise to find out what's keeping you stuck now, or in the future. Anytime you run into the pause position, take a look at this exercise and discover how to hit *play* again.

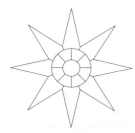

COMPASS POINTS

EXERCISE: GETTING UNSTUCK

1. Take a few moments, close your eyes, and focus on your breathing. Breathe into any area of your body that feels tight or held.

2. How does the sensation of being stuck feel in your body? (Chest feels tight, stomach is numb, neck is tense.) Use your own words to describe it.

3. Go inside yourself and ask, "What is this stuck-ness about?

   ❀ Am I afraid? If so, about what?

   ❀ Do I need help and reassurance? If so, from whom?

   ❀ Do I need information? If so, from what source?

4. What would help me unstick? Working through my fear? Time, compassion, or reaching out for support?

Remind yourself that shifting from a place of stuck-ness is a process. It can happen quickly or it may take some time. If you accept that pausing is a part of life, you lift the self-criticism and invite the self-care. That truly becomes one of the best motivators of all.

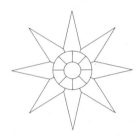

COMPASS POINTS
WEEK ONE ASSIGNMENTS

1. Do the **Four-Part Breathing** exercise daily.
2. Do the **What Does My Body Need?** exercise daily, and record your answers.
3. At the end of the week, read through your responses and see what area in your life is asking for your attention. If you are ready to make changes, read through the process-of-change checklists, make sure you are ready to do so, and have all your supports in place.
4. When you start to get answers, ask yourself, is there one step I can take this week to fulfill what my body is telling me it needs?

(((((((((Chapter Three))))))))))

Week Two:
Get Into Your Body,
Get Into Your Life

The mind can assert anything and pretend it has proved it.
My beliefs I test on my body, on my intuitional consciousness,
and when I get a response there, then I accept.

—D.H. Lawrence

Brian Wilson of the Beach Boys got the title for his group's 1966 hit, "Good Vibrations," from something his mother told him. She said that dogs could sense vibrations, and barked at people who had bad "vibes." I witnessed that behavior all the time, when I walked dogs for a living. They would use their keen instinct and respond to perceived threats that were unseen by me. Whether it was a poodle, golden retriever, Chihuahua, or Doberman, if my canine clients didn't like what they saw, they started making noise.

Can we sense good or bad vibrations as well? Yes, we can. We can use our innate instinct and intuition to discern many things about a person, place, or situation. Even if we are not always aware of our abilities, that does not mean we are incapable of using our insight. We just need to connect to it by forming a partnership with our bodies. When we do, we can then hear our inner voice and use it for decisions large and small. We don't always listen, but that doesn't stop the body from speaking. Whether it's butterflies in the stomach, a relaxing of the shoulders, or a tight feeling in the chest, the body will express how it feels. When you *do* listen, you will have access to a powerful resource. I have witnessed how empowered people feel when they start trusting their body's sensations.

When you learn to trust your body's reactions, you can start relying on its impressions about people and events in your life. In the way our animal friends use their primal instinct to sense danger or safety, you can work with yours as well. You do this by noticing how your body responds to a variety of circumstances. When you tried the **Good Feelings/ Bad Feelings** exercise in the opening chapter, you saw that your body has a definite response to a variety of positive or negative images.

Honoring your body's knowledge brings to mind a phrase I share with my dear friend and therapy colleague, Amy Torres. The phrase is, "I know what I know 'cause I feel what I feel," and we use it with each other and our clients. What we mean is that most people know, really deep down *know*, when something feels right to them. A great way to *feel what you feel* and *know what you know* is to use your body as a compass.

As you learned in Week One, reconnecting to your body's wisdom is a process. You need to warm up your body's natural energy and notice the signals you are receiving. Then you use that information to help make decisions. You want to make choices based on the best "vibrations," and once you start using that knowledge, you will feel more present and balanced in your life. By combining your body's wisdom with your natural intelligence, you will feel more in harmony—just like the classic Beach Boy song.

So how do you warm up your body's natural energy? By actively engaging it and noticing the sensations and signals it sends out. Through a series of exercises, you are going to work with your body and start exploring the messages you receive. Those messages can change the course of your life.

INNER DREAMS

For five years, Katie had been working as an administrative assistant in a large entertainment company. She was good at her job, in which she reported to a handful of bosses and attended to their many needs. She was organized, friendly, and often worked extra hours to make sure things ran smoothly during the week. In fact, Katie's sense of professional responsibility extended to everyone she came in contact in her life. The only person left out of the equation was the one in the most need: Katie herself.

Katie had a dream of being a cabaret singer. It wasn't a farfetched idea, because before her "day job," she had performed in different theaters across the country. At some point, she decided she needed more financial stability and chose to work in an office. For a while her choice was the right one because she was able to catch up on her bills. In time, the routine and lack of fulfillment in her job caused her to feel as though she was sleepwalking through life. Katie was working at an entertainment company while longing to be an entertainer herself.

Katie's body expressed the imbalance. Her jaw was constantly tight, her stomach was tense, and she struggled at times with eating too much candy. As I pointed out in Week One, when we hold back our natural expression, it has to go somewhere else in the body. Katie's "somewhere" showed up in her stomach aches and jaw tension. Her body was complaining that the singer needed to sing, and her candy cravings showed the lack of sweetness in her life.

With great determination and courage, Katie decided to explore what her body was saying to her. She started to pay close attention to how it reacted every chance she got. She noticed how lifeless her body felt when she sat at her desk and how energized she felt when she had her singing lessons. Katie saw that when she took steps to nurture her creative expression, her candy consumption dropped. As we explored her desire to sing, she continued to listen to her inner voice. With compassion, she took the time to understand her fears and then created a plan to find a singing gig that matched who she was and where she was in life. I'm happy to say that Katie now earns a living as a cabaret singer on luxury cruise lines. She walked away from a job that no longer fit and let her body-mind connection help make the transition to one that did.

WAKING UP THE BODY

To help people just like Katie get their hearts and heads in synch, I use a five-point strategy. I have found that using one or all of these techniques will help you connect to your body. The strategies are Breath, Sound, Movement, Touch, and Talk.

Breath

The first strategy used to connect you to your body is your breath. You've been doing the **Four-Part Breathing** exercise and combining it with the **What Does My Body Need?** exercise. Now I'm going to have you try two other types of breathing exercises.

How we breathe—or don't—reflects our emotional condition. Maybe you have had the experience of breathing rapidly when you are confronted with an emergency, literally holding your breath while waiting for information, and then sighing with relief when things are alright. Each stage of breathing vividly reflects our emotional state.

Your breathing actually reveals quite a bit of information, such as whether the breath flows freely from your chest to your abdomen, or is stuck in your upper chest or lower stomach. As you learned in Chapter Two, when you do not breathe fully, it's usually because you are physically compensating for something you are not allowing yourself to express.

As you observe your own breathing, you will have the opportunity to see how much you allow yourself to breathe. You are going to notice where in your body you might be holding your breath, and then, without judgment, learn to breathe a little more deeply into those areas. We'll look at two types of breathing exercises you can use to either calm you down or get you energized, depending on your need. As you start to work with both, you'll discover that the power of connecting to your breathing cannot be underestimated.

Catching your breath and utilizing all your air creates the energy you need to live your life more fully.

The first breathing exercise, **The Energizer**, is breathing that is done with an open mouth. It helps rev your metabolism, and can be used when you are feeling lethargic. Without realizing it, it's probably the type of breathing you do when you are doing some form of aerobic exercise. This open-mouth breathing brings more energy to the body and is also a great way for you to discover where you might be restricting your breathing.

The second breathing exercise, **Calm Down**, is one you can use when you are feeling anxiety or stress. It will help you relax when life feels overwhelming, and is done by *inhaling through the nose* and *exhaling through the mouth*. This type of breathing allows you to feel less frazzled and more in charge, and is good for soothing your soul when you need to quiet your emotions.

Take a quick look at yourself in the mirror before you try each of these breathing exercises.

COMPASS POINTS
Exercise: The Energizer

1. Sit comfortably with your eyes closed. Breathe normally and simply observe how the air goes in and out of your body. If there are any areas in your body where the air doesn't flow easily, make a note of it in your mind.

2. Now, inhale deeply through your mouth and slowly exhale through your mouth. Inhale deeply through your mouth again, and slowly exhale through your mouth. Repeat inhaling and slowly exhaling four times.

3. Stop and let your breathing return to normal.

4. Open your eyes, and if there is a mirror handy, take a look at yourself. See if you notice any difference in your features: more color or energy in your face, more alertness in your eyes, or less tension overall. Write down your observations.

You might find yourself feeling a little lightheaded during this exercise, and if so, stop and let your breathing return to normal. You also might find yourself wanting to stretch or move your hands and feet. Allow yourself to do so, because this breathing exercise creates more energy in the body, and it needs an outlet.

COMPASS POINTS
Exercise: Calm Down

1. Sit comfortably on a chair or the floor with your eyes closed. Let yourself breathe normally and simply observe how the air goes in and out of your body. If there are areas in your body where the air doesn't flow easily, make a note of it.

2. Now, inhale deeply through your nose and slowly exhale through your mouth. Again, inhale deeply through your nose and slowly exhale through your mouth. Do this slowly and see what you notice after each inhale and exhale. Do this exercise five times.

3. Open your eyes and look in a mirror. See if you notice any difference in your features, such as less tension in the forehead, eyes, or anywhere else. How does your body feel after doing this exercise? Write down your observations.

When you do this exercise, you might find yourself feeling a little sleepy, or fighting yawns. That's normal. Just continue to focus on your breathing and let yourself yawn or stretch in any way you need to. You also might find your mind drifting or feel a sense of time slowing down. Allow yourself to go with it, because this exercise does facilitate relaxation in the body.

Sound

The second strategy used to connect to your body's instinct and intuition is sound. Using sound and incorporating it into your life can be challenging and exciting. The challenge is that sometimes people have a fear of being heard, and struggle to connect to their actual voices. They have learned or been taught to keep quiet, and feel embarrassed about making any noise. This makes it harder for them to speak up about things that are important or to say no when they want to. Yet, getting in touch with your real voice, the inside and outside one, is empowering.

Using the power of your voice reminds me of my friend Marie and a professional breakthrough she had. Marie was a consultant in the healthcare industry, and needed to part company with a client with whom she'd been working for a number of years. Her main reason for discontinuing her association with this client was that the client refused to address some major psychological issues that were keeping her in an unhealthy place physically and emotionally. After numerous attempts to address this sensitive issue, Marie realized that her ability to support this client had reached an end point. She described to me how she knew. "I felt this physical heaviness wash over me every time I had an appointment with her, which let me know I no longer wanted to go," she said.

Marie was nervous, but told me she had to "find her voice" and stop the sessions with her client. "I have to speak up, because I feel the emotional weight in my body of not letting my voice out." When she finally did tell her client in an honest, gentle manner, that their work together was finished, the relief Marie felt was palpable. She called me on the phone and was exuberant in how free her body felt by speaking up and taking care of herself. I could hear and even feel it from her, over the phone.

Speaking up can help you reclaim or let go of areas of your life that are no longer necessary. That's the exciting part of this strategy—it's about learning to trust the power of your own voice. Here are two ways to practice.

This first exercise can be linked with either of the two breathing exercises. Try practicing them both ways.

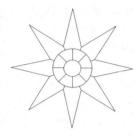

COMPASS POINTS

EXERCISE: SOUND IT OUT

1. Sit comfortably, with your eyes closed. Let yourself breathe normally and simply observe how the air goes in and out of your body. Notice if there are any areas in your body where the air doesn't flow easily, and, if you can, let yourself breathe a little more into those areas.

2. Take a deep breath in through the nose or mouth.

3. On the exhale, let out a long sighing sound. Aaaah.

4. Inhale again, and make the same sighing sound for the whole time you exhale.

5. Stop, and let your breathing return to normal.

6. Now, inhale through the nose, and on the exhale make any sound you want. See what wants to come out.

7. When you are ready, open your eyes and write down your observations. Make note of the sound you made on your own and what emotion it may have been expressing.

In this exercise you may notice things like your chest vibrating or that your voice sounds a little rusty. Just keep making whatever sound you want when you exhale, and use it to express whatever you are feeling in that moment. You could say *ah*, or you could sigh, or even hum. If you feel like making it louder, make it louder. This is your time to express the different sounds that are inside you.

This next sound exercise is much more spontaneous and free-flowing. I named it **Karaoke** because you make sound alongside something else. You make sound whenever you can, and it gives you room to hide under the radar as you practice.

COMPASS POINTS
EXERCISE: KARAOKE

Whenever you are in the car or in the shower, running a vacuum, listening to the radio, or using a blender, just allow yourself to sing, hum, and shout. You can say yes or no as loud as you want, and no one has to hear you.

That's it. That's the exercise. Use the noise of the vacuum or radio, or the fact of the windows being shut in the car to practice getting your sound out. The more you let out your voice, even if you tuck it under another sound so no one else can hear, the more you will get used to it. Even though you don't have to formally schedule this exercise, try to fit it in at least three times a week.

Movement

The next strategy is movement. When you move, there are lots of opportunities to express and release whatever is causing you emotional or physical stress. Besides exercise, there are other kinds of movement you do of which you might not be aware. People constantly tap their feet, wiggle their ankles, and roll their necks when they feel things. That's the body's nonverbal way of expressing what's going on inside. I want you to start noticing your foot-tapping, ankle-wriggling, or neck-rolling, and see if you can find out what your body is telling you. Do you shake your foot when you are feeling nervous or wring your hands when you are afraid to speak up? These are movement clues that you can start to pay attention to. Similar to Katie, the more you can attune yourself to your body's response, the more your inner voice will emerge.

Knowing how you naturally move, and the different types of movement to which you are drawn, will help you reclaim your body. You probably engage in different kinds of physical activity because it makes you feel good. Maybe it takes a few minutes to feel that sense of wellbeing, but eventually your mood responds, or else you wouldn't continue.

Knowing which movements and exercises you are drawn to at a particular time in your life also provides personal information for you. When you allow yourself to go with the type of moment you want to, you affirm the instinctive part of you that knows what's best. That's how it was for Susan.

Susan was going through a painful divorce that alternately caused her great sadness and deep anger. One day, we were discussing her feelings, and Susan burst out and said, "I just feel furious, and I need to do something about it! Everyone tells me that I should do something like yoga to calm down. But I don't want to calm down!" I asked her, "What is your body telling you it wants to do?" Susan sat for a moment and then said emphatically, "I want to do kickboxing! I want to just kick and punch and get these feelings out!" "So do it," I said. And she did. She found a kickboxing class, attended regularly, and felt relieved and empowered after every class.

Susan did what felt *right* for her, not what she thought she *should* do or what others thought she should do. She instinctively felt that her body needed to move in an assertive way. In time you'll notice this as well. You'll find that different periods in your life will have you moving in different ways. Sometimes you'll want a quieter energy when you move, and other times you will want to feel energized.

How can you tell what is the right movement for you? First, take the time to ask, and second, try it on. If you are drawn to yoga, swimming, walking, or dancing, then try them. If boxing, martial arts, or rock climbing attracts you, go for it. The activity can either help you work out something emotionally, or it can just be for sheer enjoyment. To gauge whether it's right for you, notice how you feel during and after. You want to feel a sense of pleasure and release in your body when you are done. And if you try something and you don't feel calmer, energized, or simply more relaxed, then allow yourself to explore something else.

Remember, all movement counts. As my friend Rochelle Rice, a movement specialist, says, "Movement is movement and does not have to be related at all to the usual fitness or gym environment. It's happening all the time." So walking to work, pushing a stroller, and dancing in your living room will get your energy going. When that starts to happen, you will feel more connected to your body and your inner voice.

This next exercise can be linked with either of the two breathing exercises. And remember, you can try them both together or one at a time.

COMPASS POINTS

EXERCISE: MY MOVEMENT

1. Sit comfortably, with your eyes closed. Let yourself breathe normally and simply observe how the air goes in and out of your body. Notice if there are any areas in your body where the air doesn't flow easily, and breathe a little more deeply into those areas. Then let your breathing return to normal and keep your eyes closed.

2. Starting at the top of your head, slowly focus on the different parts of your body, area by area. See if you can notice how your neck, arms, torso, hips, lower body, legs, and feet feel in this moment.

3. Now ask yourself: Where do my muscles feel tense or relaxed? What parts of my body feel as though they need to move? How does my body want to move? Go with whatever comes to mind.

4. Take a few deep breaths, open your eyes, and write down your observations.

Even if you have been in a regular exercise routine, see if you can let yourself try what your body has told you it wants to do a least once.

Touch

The simple act of touch is a powerful strategy for waking up your body's energy. Touch provides comfort, relieves stress, and offers healing. We've all had the experience of placing our hand on the shoulder of someone who is upset, or receiving a hug when we've been sad. More than the most eloquent words, those small gestures can provide great support and solace. The contact seems to give us permission to feel not only our bodies, but also our emotions. I have watched people struggle against strong feelings and only release them when they are given physical comfort. I've also seen clients who had disconnected from their bodies for various psychological reasons make peace with their bodies through the healing power of touch. When we have our bodies as an ally, we keep the conduit open between body and mind.

Touch is also a great educator of what our physical shape actually is. Many people don't have a sense of what their bodies look like or feel like in realistic terms. Whether those reasons have to do with body image issues or messages we took in from others or society, gaining a tangible awareness of our physical form can be an eye-opener. I know it was for me.

When I was growing up, my mother used to say to me, "You resemble your father's side of the family. You have short legs and a long torso." And because that was my mother's interpretation and I had no one to contradict it, I accepted her view. I took that message in and incorporated it into the picture I had formed of my body. I became, in my own mind, a person with short legs and a long torso. Done deal. Then, about eight years ago I had a reality-changing moment working with a personal trainer.

We were working on some leg exercises and she said, "I need to adjust the equipment, because your legs are long." I remember looking at her in amazement, so much so that she stopped and asked me what I was thinking. I told her my mother's version of my legs, and she laughed. She said, "Karol, I work with people of all shapes and sizes, and I can tell you from experience, you don't have short legs." She then stood next to me in front of a mirror, and with her hands, showed me the distance of my hips to my knees and my knees to my feet.

Now, I realize that I don't have legs like my friend Lillian, a former Radio City Rockette, but my image of what I did have changed completely on that day. By focusing on the visual image of my body and having my trainer lightly touch the different points on my legs, I was able to see that my old beliefs were inaccurate.

How about you? Do you have some outdated perceptions about your own body? Take a look at this checklist to see.

COMPASS POINTS
BODY PERCEPTION CHECKLIST

* Think about the way you view your own body.
* What messages were you given about your body or features?
* Who gave them to you?
* What perceptions do you have about certain body parts?

❁ What do you say to yourself automatically when you focus on that body part?

❁ When was the last time you got a reality check about your perception of a particular part of your body? (Looked in the mirror, or asked a trusted friend or loved one.)

❁ Is what you have believed all these years really accurate?

❁ What would it be like to let go of the belief?

❁ How does your body feel when you imagine doing so?

❁ What's one new message you could practice saying to yourself this week about your body? (My hair is nice, lips are pretty, arms are graceful.)

Besides getting a reality check, using and receiving touch will teach you the real shape of your body. It's a concrete way to relate to your physical form, and makes it harder to distort your perception. For some of you, the thought of being touched by another person can be uncomfortable or even scary. That's why self-touch techniques can be used instead. The two self-touch techniques I recommend are the **Body Pat-Down** and the **Butterfly Hug**. The **Body Pat-Down** has you lightly pat down the outside of your body from your head to your toes. This gets your energy flowing and gives you the opportunity to learn the shape of your body. The **Butterfly Hug** provides comfort when you are feeling upset and shows you that, despite everything that is going on, you and your body are still here.

If you are comfortable, outside touch is a great way to get a sense of your body and relieve stress. I often suggest that my clients who have histories of emotional neglect try outside touch if they can afford it. Not only does it help with psychological healing, but it also gets them in touch with their personal strength. Massage, therapeutic touch, Reiki, and acupuncture are some of the techniques I recommend for both healing and reality-checking. Reflexology is another healing modality that works on the whole body, yet the touch is focused on the feet. If you are not comfortable with touch, reflexology can feel less invasive than having someone touch your legs, arms, or torso, Also, if you want to try these techniques but are concerned about the cost, there are often schools for practitioners that have low-cost clinics. This allows the senior students, who are supervised by their teachers, to get the experience and hours they need to complete their education.

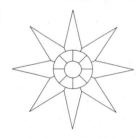

COMPASS POINTS

Exercise: Body Pat-Down

1. Stand or sit so that you are comfortable.
2. Keeping your eyes open, place your hands on the top of your head.
3. Gently start patting the outside of your head and neck.
4. Gently rub your forehead, eyebrows, temples, cheeks, nose, mouth, and chin.
5. Keep patting the outside of your neck, shoulders, and arms.

6. Reach around, if you can, and lightly pat and touch your middle and lower back.

7. Pat your chest, stomach, and belly.

8. Gently pat the outside of your hips, buttocks, thighs—back and front—knees, shins, calves, ankles, and feet.

9. Continue standing or sitting and notice any feelings or sensations in the body where you have patted yourself.

10. Take a deep breath, inhaling and exhaling.

11. Now close your eyes and do the same patting exercise again.

12. Take a deep breath and open your eyes.

13. Write down any observations you have about how your body feels here.

This next exercise is especially good for when you are feeling upset, anxious, or mentally scattered.

COMPASS POINTS
EXERCISE: BUTTERFLY HUG

1. Find a comfortable place to sit. You can have your feet on the ground, legs stretched out in front of you, or sit cross-legged. Just choose a comfortable position.

2. Close your eyes and breathe in through the nose and out through the mouth. Continue with this type of breathing three or four times.

3. Cross your arms so that your right hand is resting on your left shoulder or upper arm and your left hand is resting on your right shoulder or upper arm.

4. Give yourself a hug or squeeze, take a deep breath, and then exhale. Let your hands do any motion they want to: gently patting the tops of your shoulders or upper arms, or rubbing the tops of your shoulders or upper arms. Continue breathing in through the nose and out through the mouth as you do this hugging or patting motion.

5. When you feel calmer, open your eyes and let your arms drop down.

6. Sit for a few moments and observe how your body feels.

This exercise can be used even when you are not upset. It can be done in the car, right before you go into work. You can do it in your office to help calm you before an important meeting, or before and after you have a difficult conversation. This touch reestablishes the bond you have always had with your body, even if it got lost along the way.

If you want to try receiving outside touch, you can discover what type feels right to you by first asking your body.

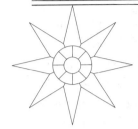

COMPASS POINTS

EXERCISE: OUTSIDE TOUCH

1. Sit comfortably, with your eyes closed.
2. Let yourself inhale and exhale normally and simply observe how the air goes in and out of your body. Let your breathing return to normal. Now ask yourself:
    * What areas of my body feel tense or tight?
    * What is my body telling me about how it wants to be touched?
    * Do I want a massage, healing session, manicure, pedicure, or reflexology? Let your answer float up to your mind.
3. Take a few deep breaths, open your eyes, and write down your observations.

Ask your trusted friends, family, and coworkers if they can recommend a practitioner they like. Have them describe why they like the person, and notice if their reasons match your own needs. Remember to try a variety of different services until you find the one that fits you best.

Talk

Experiencing words and concepts with the body, as we did with the exercise in the opening chapter, is new to many of you. Typically, when we play association games, we're asked to say whatever word comes to mind first when we are prompted by another word. In this strategy, you are going to be asked to notice "What comes to body."

Besides the physical signs and symptoms of our instinct and intuition, we also use words to describe how our bodies feel. And those words, whether we are talking to ourselves or another person, can be used to find out interesting aspects of who we are. Talk allows us to create an inner dialog from the body to the mind and gives us the information we need to take care of ourselves.

I once worked with a young woman who had worked very hard to overcome an eating disorder. She was learning how to make friends with her body again. One day, she was telling me how she was feeling, and I asked her to describe what her body was feeling as well. In other words, "What comes to body?" She said, "I feel a lot of tension in my stomach." I asked her to describe the tension for me. Because she's was a very visual person, she often used colors to illustrate her body's sensations. She said, "My stomach is gray, it's very gray and it's very dark. I asked her what the grayness meant and what the color was saying. She said, "The grayness is my self-esteem today. I feel very blah." From there we started to work with what was causing her self-esteem to be low and what was needed to shift her mood.

Some people aren't so visual, and will say things such as, "I feel tense, knotty, and heavy in my head like I'm in a storm cloud." I'll then use their words to try and find out what they mean. I'll ask, "If your tension could talk, what would it tell me?" Or, "If that heaviness had a voice, what would it want to let you know?" Talking from the body's perspective gives you the emotional information beneath the words or descriptions. Once you have that information, you will begin to understand what you need to make things better. You can then ask, "What does my body need in order for that feeling to shift?"

Talking with others is another good way to connect to what your body is saying, because there are times in our lives when we just get overwhelmed. We might have a faint sense of what we need to stay in balance, but can wind up second-guessing ourselves. Those are the times we need good, supportive people in our corner with whom we can talk things through. Later in the book, I devote an entire chapter to helping you figure out who the people are in your life you can rely on. Until then, think about the people you know. When you go over the list in your mind, whoever brings a smile to your face is usually a good bet as far as support is concerned.

To see what your body might be "saying," try the next exercise.

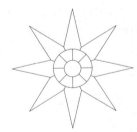

COMPASS POINTS
Exercise: Body Talk

1. Sit comfortably, with your eyes closed.
2. Let yourself breathe normally and simply observe how the air goes in and out of your body.
3. In your mind's eye, slowly scan your body from your head to your toes.
4. Now ask yourself:
    * What areas of my body feel tense, tight, or blocked?

❀   What colors, sensations, or images describe
    that area?

❀   What words can be used to translate what
    those areas are feeling?

❀   What words can be used to tell me what my
    body needs for those areas?

5. Check in on each area. When you are finished, open
   your eyes.

6. Write down your observations in your notebook.

UNEXPECTED FEELINGS

When your body begins to wake up, emotions that may
have been buried begin to emerge. You may feel lighter and
happier as you feel your body more. You also might feel other
emotions, such as sadness or anger. When the body has the
opportunity to release emotions, in order to get in balance,
it will. Picture this scenario: Imagine how you feel on a
very cold day, when you are chilled to the bone. All your
limbs feel heavy and stiff as you fight the freezing weather.
When you get inside and start to warm up, you feel almost
an ache in your muscles, because you had been holding them
so tightly to keep your heat inside. Eventually, you start to
warm up, and the soreness in your muscles starts to fade.
Your body then relaxes into a calmer state.

I use this analogy because, in addition to the instinctual
and intuitive awakening in your body, there is the possibility of emotional awakening as well. As I mentioned in
Chapter Two, the emotion-intuition link is very strong.
Does this mean you have to be feeling your feelings all the
time in order to connect to your instinct and intuition? No,
it just means that when these aspects start to get activated,
the other aspects can as well. If that occurs, and you are

confused or puzzled by what you are feeling or how your life is changing, don't hesitate to reach out for support. Whether it's a significant other, good friend, therapist, spiritual counselor, or family member; having a trusted sounding board is one of the best ways to stay aligned with your inner voice.

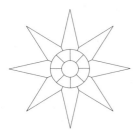

COMPASS POINTS
WEEK TWO ASSIGNMENTS

1. Continue with the **Four-Part Breathing** exercise.

2. Continue with the **What Does My Body Need?** exercise started in Week One.

3. Choose two of the body wake-up strategies to try this week. The easiest ones to take on are the breathing exercises, followed by the movement exercises. Record your responses and reactions to each strategy you try.

4. Try one body-appreciation statement this week. Write it down daily in your journal or notebook.
   OPTIONAL:

5. If you feel like really stretching yourself, tell a trusted friend or loved one the distorted beliefs you have about your body. Then share with them the new belief you are trying on.

(((((((((CHAPTER FOUR)))))))))

Week Three:
Your Professional Path

It is only by following your deepest instinct that you can lead a rich life.

—Katharine Butler Hathaway

David was confused. He had recently taken a position as a salesperson for a company that sold medical supplies. Originally an actor, he was looking to create more financial stability, and chose what he called a "safe" job. "Safe" for David meant a steady paycheck, health insurance, and knowing he could pay his bills. He also thought his people skills would be useful in sales. These were all valid reasons to take this new path, but there was one problem. After being on the job less than a month, David felt lousy. He dreaded going to work, felt a nagging knot of tension in his upper back, lacked energy, and found himself doubting his abilities. He kept asking, "What is wrong with me? I wanted more security, I got it. I needed health insurance, I have it. I wanted people contact, and I deal with them every day. But I can't stand it; I must be a very selfish person, because I'm just not satisfied."

It was easy for David to make those blanket statements about himself, because he was only using one perspective—the logic of his mind. Sure, everything looked good "on paper;" the job matched his original wish list, and if that was the measure of his happiness, he should be ecstatic. So what was the problem? If all he looked at was the criteria he required for his ideal job, then nothing. But if he went beyond the facts and widened his perspective to his body's reactions, then something was definitely off.

David dismissed the responses in his body as if they were happening outside of him, as if his body was having a bothersome tantrum while his logical mind strived to be mature and stoic. When David and I explored this issue, he discovered it wasn't such a cut-and-dry scenario, and his body knew it. Instead of disregarding his body's reaction, I suggested to David that he find out why his body was responding so strongly. He agreed to try.

What about you? Do you love your job? Hate your job? Need a change? Need a starting point? These are the questions that show up when you are making decisions about work and career. They can drive you crazy if you don't take the time to find out what your inner voice is saying.

How do we know if we are on the right track when it comes to our career choices? Many times, it's the difference between waking up with a sense of purpose and excitement or facing the day with a sense of dread and anxiety. Those are impressions you can discern in your body. As you experienced in the first exercise you tried in the opening chapter, you know your body can tell the difference between what feels good and what feels bad. So, what's your body telling you about your career or job?

LOSING YOUR WAY

Whether we are entrepreneurs, work for a company, or are struggling to find out what we want to do, finding career fulfillment is fraught with trial and error. Sometimes you can find yourself trapped in a career that you either never wanted, or had wanted at one point but have since outgrown. You may not even be aware that things are off course except for the fact that you are irritable or bored. You may find yourself handling your dissatisfaction through behaviors such as excessive drinking, eating, or shopping. If these activities are happening more and more in your life, it's important to pay attention to them. These behaviors are your body's way of telling you that something is off in your life. The tendency to turn toward body-numbing activities means something is brewing beneath the surface that you may not want to deal with. But those feelings don't go away. They will just increase in intensity. That's why it's important to listen. Such was the case with David.

When David finally consulted his body, he started to get some answers. By taking the time daily to ask the same question you learned in Week One ("What does my body need?") a persistent answer began to emerge—*creative expression*. Although it was true David's current job provided financial security, health benefits, and interpersonal contact with others, it was not really a position that matched his skill set or temperament. David was a creative guy, filled with ideas and enthusiasm. His supervisor, a moody man with a volatile temper, was not open to new methods of selling medical supplies, and his colleagues were burdened by the red tape of the company. In reality, selling medical equipment was not really the kind of interaction David envisioned when he thought about connecting with people. None of the job's aspects fit with who David really was and how the position was represented to him. Once David realized the mismatch, he was ready to address the problem. He wanted to honor his inner voice and see what steps he needed to take to find a new job that matched him more.

There are many reasons for staying in a career or job that are usually focused on financial obligations and family responsibilities. We also stay in careers because we've lost sight of what matters to us or makes us feel fulfilled. It's understandable why that could happen. We get caught up in the day-to-day routines of life and lose track of our direction. We may stay put because the thought of change is scary, and/or we doubt our abilities. Through time, we may remain where we are because we have repressed or pushed down the part of us that is creative, powerful, or incisive. When we do so, we are left feeling trapped, stuck, and out of touch with the part of us that knows when things are in balance.

CHANGING IDENTITIES

What if you've always been an accountant, artist, dancer, or lawyer? You chose a career path years ago that seemed to suit you perfectly at that time. You felt strongly about your choice and entered your field enthusiastically. Everything was going along fine, until...it wasn't. You started to feel less enthusiastic about your work. Maybe what you loved, or at least liked, doing for many years no longer seems to fit. Even if you tried to ignore it, a creeping dissatisfaction has entered the picture. Typically, it shows up as tiredness, unexplained aches in your body, or a restlessness that you can't seem to shake. For many people those signals lie under the radar, and even though they are happening, they are brushed off as symptoms of other issues. You tell yourself you just need a vacation, need to put more effort into your job, or are feeling run down because there's a bug going around the office. Or perhaps, like David, you feel as though something's wrong with you. But what if it's not you?

To contemplate a change in your career when you've been doing the same thing for a while is unsettling and, perhaps, secretly exhilarating. When I made the transition from performer to psychotherapist, it was because I was no longer satisfied by what I was doing. At first the signals were a little muffled, but in time got louder. I noticed that my mood was low when I went on auditions, and the satisfaction of working on theatrical projects was not there. I had enjoyed success as a working actress but did not have the motivation or desire to go another level. I was not sure why and took the time to explore it with a therapist. I ultimately realized that the part of performing I liked the most was when I could be myself and express my own thoughts and ideas. I liked interacting with an audience and was looking for my own voice to emerge as opposed to playing a part. What finally helped me crystallize my decision to change my career was attending a lecture by the meditation teacher and author Stephen Levine.

During his talk on spirituality, Stephen said, "Your life's work changes." I remember being startled when I heard that statement. My whole body became energized, and I felt a rush of excitement go up my spine. He went on to say that what you once loved doing in life transforms in time, and that it's important to allow those shifts to happen. He explained that the passion you felt for your original career was valid *at that time*, and to pay attention to the fact that it may have changed.

His words touched me and, on some level, gave me the permission to let go of my old career as a performer. I felt something lift off of my body, and I had a clear sense of my new identity breaking free. From that point on, my interest in psychology and communication became clearer. Then I began the journey of shedding my outdated identity.

Saying Goodbye

It took me a year to adjust to the idea that I was no longer a performer, and it was a period of sorrow, relief, and letting go. I needed to say goodbye to my old identity as a performer, and I felt its loss. After so many years of knowing exactly what to say when someone asked what I did, I now had to formulate a new answer. The same was true for Linda.

For years, Linda enjoyed tremendous success working as a professional make-up artist. Her client list was long and she was often called to work on movie projects and commercials. There were trips across the country and visits to Europe. In time, Linda started to feel drained both by her work and the travel. What used to inspire creativity now left her feeling listless and bored. She appreciated her clients and the projects she had contributed to, but she no longer felt the joy in just applying make-up. Instead, what had been growing in her heart was a desire to speak and write about her expertise in caring for the skin by choosing good facial products. Linda wanted to inspire others on how to look good and no longer wanted to do the one-on-one work anymore. She paid attention to the sensations in her body every time she went on a job, and they confirmed for her she had to change. As she let the real truth of what she now wanted in her life become more of a reality, Linda felt a sense of grief and relief. She needed to say goodbye to her old identity as a make-up artist in order to feel the joy of honoring her new path. Throughout the course of two years, she let go of clients and travel and created the space for speaking and writing.

MAKING THE TRANSITION

The theme of change shows up throughout this book. As you listen to your inner voice and see how accurate it can be, you will start to make changes. That process is unique to you and is filled with highs and lows. In regard to your professional path, it's important not to judge the feelings that may emerge around leaving one career and moving toward another. Many people worry that not being absolutely sure about the direction they are going in will slow their journey. Nothing can be further from the truth. The more you are able to share with others the doubt and fears you may have about your future, the steadier your transition will be. No single feeling is "better" than the others, and you need to allow yourself to feel the range of emotions that come up around transformation. If it were easy, we would all be making changes right and left. Often it's not. Whether you are taking a giant step forward or pausing until you figure out the next small one, treat yourself with compassion. You will need it, because sometimes you plan change and sometimes it's thrust upon you. That's what happened with Amy.

A DIFFERENT DIRECTION

Amy was stuck. Each day for the past 12 years, she had been heading to the same building, sitting at the same desk, and complaining about the same unsatisfying job. Every morning, as she got off the same elevator and walked the same long hallway to the office door, she felt like she was dying a slow, painful death. Amy's soul was dying, that was for sure. But she was also experiencing some persistent stomach trouble. She imagined she had an ulcer, except that her stomach only bothered her when she was at work.

Then Amy's destiny was decided for her—to a point. The company where she had been in a holding pattern went belly-up, so the choice of whether or not she should keep working at that job was made for her. But then what? Amy felt she was without direction and longed to find her way but was feeling hopeless. When I met Amy in a Find Your Inner Voice Goals Group, she was skeptical.

Amy had a sense that her life was off track because she was on the wrong path professionally. So even though she was doubtful, Amy began exploring a new career by following a hunch she'd had years earlier. She had always dreamed of opening up an art studio where children could come after school and work on creative projects. But after so many years of "going through the motions," she had all but forgotten her dream.

Amy began to notice and use the intuitive messages that her body was giving her every time she imagined herself in her new career. Those of us in the group could see it too. Her eyes lit up, she sat up taller, and spoke in a joyful manner about working with art. Using her body signals as a compass, she planned out the steps of her new career. Soon, her whole world began to open up and her professional life got on track. She finally felt the strength to move forward and take the steps needed to fulfill her dream.

MIND YOUR BODY

Amy's journey toward the right career path involved forming a relationship with her body that was different from before. Like many of you, Amy had exercised and moved for health reasons but had not had the experience of noticing what her body was telling her in regard to her personal happiness. You can find a way to tune in to the signals of your body and understand their meaning in regard to your career fulfillment as well. Waking up your instinctive body is about getting your energy flowing, asking the questions, and then paying attention to the answers. Right after Amy attended the Find Your Inner Voice seminar, she started up her small business. Even though she had no idea if it would be able to sustain itself, she now considers herself a success— something that having an unsatisfying career had prevented her from knowing before.

Take a moment to go through these questions regarding your career and see what your body has to say.

COMPASS POINTS
BODY BAROMETER CAREER CHECKLIST

❈ What does your body feel like when you imagine going to work?

❈   Where do you feel the sensations specifically?

❈   How long have you felt this way? (Days, months, years.)

❈   When you imagine remaining in this position, how does your body feel? (Excited, inspired, sad, burdened.)

❈   When you imagine leaving, how does your body feel? (Joyful, relieved, unhappy, energized.)

If you got the sense that you are right where you should be in your career, then keep going. If you got the feeling that you need to be somewhere else, don't worry, there are exercises at the end of this chapter to help get you pointed in the right direction.

EVERYTHING COUNTS

Even if you know that it's time to let go of your current career, you don't want to forget your past. All the skills you have acquired throughout the years will count in the future. You will tap into those abilities in unexpected ways and use them with ease, because you have developed the experience to do so. My friend Jeanette Bronée, who is a holistic health counselor, utilized her skills as a former interior designer to create her new office space. Not only is it one of the nicest offices in which to meet her clients, but she artistically designed her company logo and Website as well.

Similarly, I never would have thought it, but my previous experience working in restaurants turned out to be a valuable resource for me. I had been asked by financial planner to coach her on a speech she was giving to a group of women business owners. Not only was she speaking, but she also was in charge of planning the event. When I met her at the location where the party was to be held, I ended up not only coaching her on her presentation, but also organizing where the food, chairs, and bar were to be set up. She was extremely grateful for the support and her presentation was stronger for it. I was happy that those years of waiting tables and catering finally paid off. Embrace your past accomplishments, as the experience gained will provide the building blocks for your new career. You will use them to great effect when you least expect to.

WHICH WAY TO GO

Imagine walking through the woods on a sunny day. As you stroll along, you get caught up in the scenery and lose track of time. Suddenly the landscape doesn't look as familiar, and you aren't sure of where you are. A sense of worry sets in as you try to figure out where you came from and what direction to take. Things start to blend together and you become confused. At this point, if you had a compass, you would pull it out and get your bearings. But if you didn't, you could use your body compass instead. You would slow down, catch your breath, connect to your five senses, and let them guide you. Taking the time to use your senses would help you find familiar cues from the environment. You would hear the sound of water, which reminds you of the creek you were following. You would see where the sun is shining through the trees and feel its warmth from where it is hanging in the sky. You might hear the sound of other hikers and follow their voices to get you back on your path.

When we become overwhelmed in life, we start to operate out of panic and confusion. We circle round and round decisions and get trapped in the logic of our minds. Taking the time to calm down and listen to your body helps you navigate your way through life's choices. This all comes back to the body-mind connection. Once you are familiar with your inner compass, it becomes easier to rely on it again and again to achieve what you want.

ADVOCATING SUCCESS WITH INSTINCT

Ashley owns her own milliner business. For many years, she had worked steadily on her career while holding down a 9-to-5 job. She loved creating her knitted hats and crocheted earrings, so it wasn't a waste of time for her, but she often thought that once her business started making a profit she could leave her day job. Ashley knew how to make beautiful items, but she didn't know how to sell them as well as she wanted. But that was soon to change.

At an outdoor craft event, the manager of the show assigned Ashley to a spot that, according to her, "just felt wrong for me to have my hats there." This wasn't a new feeling for Ashley, this experience of sensing that things were wrong. Previously, when she'd had those sensations she didn't do anything about them. She had always ignored the feeling of unease in her stomach that sometimes accompanied the imperfect positioning of her merchandise at other events. The results? She didn't sell many hats. But things were about to change.

Mulling over the same stomach signals she was getting about being assigned to the lousy spot, Ashley decided to take a walk around the craft show. "That's when I noticed an empty booth that felt perfect to display my stuff," she told me. "When I saw it, I had a very positive feeling about it, a tingling on my neck. I could see myself in it, surrounded by my hats. I knew exactly how they would be arranged in this space, unlike the one I had been assigned to. I also saw myself happily selling most of my merchandise." The feeling in her body and the vision she saw caused her to act.

Ashley sought the person running the event and asked about the second booth she had seen. Turned out it was available due to a cancellation by the person who had booked it. Ashley asked to take the booth, and told me "it was the best thing I ever did." That day, she sold more of her hats than ever before. She recalled that it felt right: the booth, the selling, and the customers' response to her work. She finally came to the deep realization that creating and selling her designs was her passion and destiny.

When I asked Ashley what it felt like *in her body* to have the booth choice feel "right," she thought for a moment and explained: "I felt an excitement, a glow. Like energy is flowing through my whole body." Ashley experienced this feeling of pleasure, which made her realize that everything was right with her and the world. By noticing her body and visualizing her success, she was able to take the initiative and move to a more desirable location.

Have you had this experience yourself? Can you picture doing what you want, even if it hasn't happened yet? Many of us do it unconsciously when we dream about the future. But we write off our visions as fantasies, which prevents us from taking a second look. Some of the things we dream about are grandiose and may never happen. Yet the essence of those fantasies provides us with the clues we need for future choices. My fantasy of being a Broadway dancer is not going to happen at this point, but the joy of dance is something I create in my life by taking jazz classes. When I am dancing, it feels "right" in my body, and I picture myself being creative in other areas of my life. Ashley did the same, and that's how she, using her body compass, found her "True North."

YOUR TRUE NORTH

The moment you find your own True North you will experience feelings of either intense excitement or deep calmness. No matter what the feeling, most people describe the energy in their body as "moving" or "flowing." Like Ashley, they finally feel in alignment with who they are. They find their right direction and are able to experience clarity in decision-making. They know what they want, when it feels "right," and how to advocate for themselves in order to get it.

How can you find your True North? The first step to take is finding in your body where you feel the same kind of excitement or empowerment that Ashley did that day. She followed her instinct about her original location, and acted on her vision. From that point on she trusted her body and knew she was on the right path, not only at the craft show, but in life.

The way to find your True North is through the body-mind connection. Accessing your body-mind connection involves understanding and reconnecting with your five basic senses. These senses are the gateways to your inner self. By stimulating and refreshing your ability to use your senses, you open up your awareness to inner and outer information. This allows you to use all the capabilities your body has to offer.

The following exercise will help you find the place of knowing in your body. You will visit each of your senses and see how responsive they truly are. Having them active will aid your body's ability to figure out your direction when you need to.

Have your journal or notebook and a pen on hand.

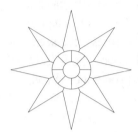

COMPASS POINTS

EXERCISE: FIND YOUR TRUE NORTH

1. Take a few moments to sit quietly with your hands in your lap.
2. Think about your five senses. To which of these do you respond the strongest? Is it taste?
3. Does touch, either receiving or giving, make you feel a certain way?
4. Do sounds evoke physical reactions?
5. What about what you see or smell? Chances are, you rely on one of these more than the others, but all come into play in some way or other. For this exercise choose one and focus on it.

TASTE

Picture the most delicious, satisfying taste you can imagine—Mom's chicken soup, Dad's chili, your favorite dessert, homemade lemonade, or whatever appeals to you the most. Imagine yourself taking a taste, savoring the flavor as it rolls over your tongue. As you imagine yourself enjoying the flavor and texture of your favorite food or beverage, pay attention to how your body responds. Focus on the physical sensation this pleasurable activity gives to you. Write your observations in your journal.

TOUCH

Think about the most relaxing, stimulating, or otherwise pleasurable touch you can ever remember feeling—the softest cashmere gliding against your skin, the warm hands of your significant other, a comforting hug, a sumptuous bath, holding your child in your arms. As you imagine yourself enjoying the caress, the security, the softness of the touch, pay attention to how your body feels. Focus on the physical sensations and record what you notice in your journal.

SOUND

Imagine the sounds that make your energy level rise or fall, like a piece of music that energizes and inspires, or one that calms you. Perhaps a sound that really resonates with you is the crashing of ocean waves, the tinkle of wind chimes, the rustling of leaves, the contented purring of your cat as she naps on your lap, the laugh of your child. Really focus on the sound you chose, imagining it as if you were hearing it right at this moment. How does your body respond? Record the physical sensations you experience in your journal.

SIGHT

Picture the sights that make you feel joyful—a night sky dotted with thousands of stars, snowflakes falling and dusting the trees, the smile of your significant other. With your imagination, visualize an original place where all that you love and hold dear are within view. Focus on your body as you see this world before you and notice how your body feels when you take it all in. Record the sensations you feel in your journal.

SMELL

Think about scents that evoke emotion in you, making you feel happy, content, energized, robust—a spicy cologne or delicate perfume, the tantalizing smell of cookies baking, a fresh bouquet of your favorite flowers, leaves burning in a bonfire. Imagine yourself experiencing an aroma that brings you pleasure. Notice how that scent affects your physical body and record what you feel in your journal.

Once you've completed the exercise, really look at your answers. Were you able to describe sensations in your body for each or all of your senses? By practicing this exercise you wake up your body's amazing ability to give you information. As you become more alive in body and mind, you are well on your way to finding your own True North.

YOUR PERSONAL VALUES

Now that you have activated your inner compass, it's time to find out what matters to you. Doing so either affirms the professional path you are on or starts you on exploring other avenues. The way to do this is by looking at your core values. Your core values are the inner qualities that are most important to you. Core values define who you are and what you stand for. The significance of knowing what your values are is that you give yourself more opportunities to:

* Honor yourself.
* Increase your satisfaction and sense of your life's meaning.
* Create personal and professional fulfillment.

Once you know your values, you can plan your time and design your life to live more fully from your ideals. You will start to know when things feel "off" if your standards are not being honored. Knowing inside and out what is meaningful to you is critical for making choices. Your core values become additional compass points for decision-making. You need to be clear about what your values are and not define them on what they *should be* according to an outside definition.

For example, if one of your core values is "family" but an ongoing work requirement keeps you from spending time at home, this becomes a stressful factor for you. If the job situation is permanent, it will affect your family life because a value that is important to you is being dishonored. The stress of being out of sync with your core values produces internal emotional clutter, and your body will reflect the conflict. You may feel distracted or irritable, or develop a host of body aches and pains. These are indicators that you are in conflict with yourself.

Not all of us can walk away from every uncomfortable work position we have, but identifying your values will help you uncover and understand more of who you are. Then you can check in with the standards that resonate with you and negotiate to the best of your ability within your job. Let's take a look at your core values in this next exercise.

In this exercise you will be using both your mind and body. You will be looking at a list of words that register in your mind. Then you will choose and circle as many of the words to which you are instinctively drawn. You can add any words of your own, if they are not on the list.

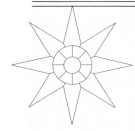

COMPASS POINTS
Exercise: Core Values

Without over-thinking, circle the words that speak to you.

Art	Service	Discovery
Teaching	Advocacy	Creativity
Beauty	People	Nature
Community	Leadership	Success
Adventure	Spirituality	Emotion
Ambition	Freedom	Family
Love	Movement	Empathy
Courage	Integrity	Communication
Performing	Writing	Stillness
Joy	Structure	Healing
Excitement	Animals	Passion
Wealth	Harmony	Loyalty
Fun	Health	Knowledge

From this list, write down the five words that are the most meaningful to you. Ask yourself how your body feels when you focus on each word you have chosen.

Word: Body Sensation

(Any physical sensation, where you feel it in your body, and so on.)

1. Communication: chest is warm, excitement in stomach

2.

3.

4.

5.

These are your core value and compass points. They are the signposts that will guide you personally and professionally. On a regular basis, and especially when you have to make important decisions, ask yourself if you are honoring the values that are the most meaningful to you. In the following checklist, you will explore whether these values are in your life right now.

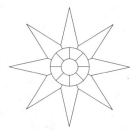

COMPASS POINTS
MY VALUES CHECKLIST

* ❋ Are you honoring your values in your life right now?
* ❋ Where in your life are you ignoring your values?
* ❋ If you were to honor your values, what would be different in your life right now?
* ❋ Post a list of your values where you can refer to them—your desktop, bulletin board, refrigerator, and so on.

PICTURING THE FUTURE

When you use your imagination and picture the future, you open yourself up to possibilities. When clients do this, they often tell me that opportunities matching their vision for the future start to cross their path. They run into people that offer information about the new field they are considering, or they hear three people mention an idea they were contemplating. I find it's like that radio signal I mentioned:

as you activate the body-mind connection, you pick up on more information you may not have noticed before. The best part is you will have your True North to rely on when you need to make a decision.

COMPASS POINTS

EXERCISE: PICTURING THE FUTURE

1. Sit comfortably in a chair or on the floor.
2. Close your eyes.
3. Do the **Four-Part Breathing** exercise.
4. Visualize what you would like to study or do for a living if there were no obstacles. What would it be? If it's more than one thing, just focus on one thing for now. (If you can't get a picture, ask yourself what aspects of life bring you joy or contentment.)
5. Imagine yourself in this career or job, or doing this course of study. Be specific about the detail. Where you would be? In what way would you would be involved?
6. When you have the picture in your mind, just focus on it.
7. How do you know this choice makes you feel happy or content?
8. Where do you feel it and sense it in your body? Identify the places.
9. How does your energy feel when you visualize yourself in this activity, career, or class?

10. Now take a deep breath.

11. Bring to your mind doing the opposite of what you want. This could be anything that does not make you feel content, satisfied, or joyful. (It could be what you are doing now.)

12. Focus on this picture.

13. How does your body and energy feel?

14. Where do you feel it?

15. Take a deep breath and let the image go.

16. Now go back to the earlier picture of the career, profession, or study that makes you feel excited and alive.

17. How does your energy feel?

18. Where do you feel those places in your body that know it is right?

19. Without thinking, just answer this question: What do you think blocks you from this goal?

20. What's one action you could take to unblock yourself?

21. What one small step are you willing to take to see this happen?

22. Take a few deep breaths, and open your eyes.

23. Write down your observations in your journal.

As with all change, making the decision to shift your career path is a big deal. Whether you are redefining your current position or leaving a long-held occupation, it's important to take the time you need to make it happen. Use all the supports and tools you have identified in previous weeks, such as the **Personality Style Checklist**, **Life Circumstances Checklist**, and the **Achievement Validation**

Checklist, from Week One. Later on you will be able to use an exercise in Week Four (Chapter Five) that will be helpful. This is an example of how you can blend different aspects of this book to work together.

COMPASS POINTS
Week Three Assignments

1. Continue with **Four-Part Breathing** on daily basis.

2. Continue with the **What Does My Body Need?** exercise.

3. If you are working: For this week, pay attention to how your body feels when you go into your job. If you notice that your energy does not feel good, make sure you look at the **Core Values** exercise and see if yours are being represented. If not:

   ❁ Do the **Picturing the Future** exercise daily and record your answers for the week.

   ❁ Read your answers at the end of the week and see what shows up on a regular basis.

4. If you are not working:

   ❁ Do the **Core Values** exercise.

   ❁ Do the **Picturing the Future** exercise daily and record your answers for the entire week.

   ❁ Read your answers at the end of the week and see what responses are showing up consistently.

❋   Start listing any careers that match those
     answers.

❋   Ask yourself if there is one step you are willing
     to take to explore those careers. (Work on
     resume, ask others about the field, research
     online.)

❋   Who can you call, meet with, or discuss with
     any of the steps you want to take regarding
     your career? Make a list of three to five people
     and schedule some time to get together.

(((((((((CHAPTER FIVE)))))))))

Week Four:
Friends and Otherwise

If we look honestly at our relationships, we can see so much about how we have created them.

—Shakti Gawain

"It's too much work! Every time the phone rings and I see that it's Heather, I get this pit in my stomach." My client Linda was upset because she was feeling this way about a supposed friend. They'd been friends for about five years, and Linda felt their friendship had deteriorated in the past few years. She and Heather had met at a previous job and stayed in touch socially after Linda left the company. "It's always the same when we go out. She wants to meet men, and when we go anywhere, she ends up ignoring me when someone she is interested in starts talking to us. I've brought it up to her, but she tells me I'm too serious and

that it's not a big deal. But it is a big deal! She says I'm
overreacting when she's not on time or cancels at the last
minute." I asked Linda to explain what the pit in her stomach was saying to her when her friend would call. She sat a
moment, and then said, "My gut knows I can't be who I
want to be when I'm with her." When I asked how it would
feel felt on a body level to not have Heather in her life.
Linda paused, took a deep breath and said, "I would feel a
little sad, like letting go of something, but I also feel a sense
of relief in my chest. I don't think we've had a real friendship for a long time."

Throughout the next few months, Linda and I worked
on the reasons she felt obligated to stay in her friendship
until she understood what she wanted to do. She tried again
to resolve her conflict with Heather, who continued not to
respond, and Linda chose to gradually not be so available.
Eventually the two friends stopped spending time together.
Linda felt freer in her body and did not have that pit in her
stomach whenever the phone rang.

Our connection to other people comes in all different
forms. There are family relationships, personal friendships,
work friends, neighbors, and the day-to-day interactions
we have with strangers. These connections can either support or drain us, depending on with whom we choose to
spend time. Some relationships are based on history, shared
interests, or chemistry. Some relationships are vital and en-
ergizing, and others are sustained out of habit—even
though they no longer feel good for us. This week, we are
going to look at how you can evaluate your platonic relationships to see if they are still a good fit.

What is your body telling you about the people with
whom you spend time? Probably quite a bit. I'm sure there

are relationships in your life that make you feel terrific and happy. Those are the particular friends, family members, and colleagues whom you love to be around and with whom you share the details of your life. These are the ones you feel cared for, inspired, and supported by. You are aware of the warm, happy energy in your body when you spend time with them. There are also those special individuals who tell it like it is, when you need the honesty. All these different relationships add to your sense of community and connection to others.

With some relationships, it is often easy to avoid the other, not-so-nice sensations rumbling around in your body. The feelings that occur when someone with whom you spend time does not make you feel uplifted, respected, or supported. In fact, you feel quite the opposite. These are the people in your life who create the same feelings of dread that Linda felt. With some of those relationships, we tend to override our body's messages. We either develop a blind spot to how we are being affected, or tolerate feeling uncomfortable. This can be puzzling. Why would we continue to spend time with people who do not makes us feel good when we are around them? Let's look at some of the causes.

FAMILY DYNAMICS

We choose people to be in our lives based on our early family dynamics. Those relationships could either have been positive or negative. Maybe you grew up with loving parents, distant parents, or in a more extreme dynamic involving alcoholism, substance abuse, or violence. These familial behaviors, loving or not, have a long-lasting impact on our lives.

From our primary caregivers, we form many of our ideas about how people relate to each other. We learned how to behave with others by observing the way parents and other adults acted in front of us, day in and day out. Like a sponge, you absorb the verbal and nonverbal behaviors that are modeled for you. When you become an adult, you tend to go out into the world and re-create the family you grew up with. You probably are not even aware of doing so. Yet, we do tend to duplicate what we know in our relationships, even if the familiar is not so good for us.

HABITUAL ROLES

Lisa, the youngest child in her family, had always felt as though she was a burden. Her father, a kind but troubled man, struggled with alcoholism. Her mother worked long hours to keep the family afloat and was often weary. With six children in total, there wasn't a lot of time spent on Lisa's emotional needs.

Because her mother was overwhelmed and her father's presence was inconsistent, Lisa didn't feel that there was a lot of room for her emotional needs. When she did try to get her mother's attention, she felt her mother's exhaustion, and always thought she was asking for too much.

Lisa carried physical tension in her body, mainly in her upper back and shoulders. She felt her body was always braced against ongoing disappointment. Lisa admitted that she usually stayed in the background when she was with others and tried to handle everything on her own. She struggled with overeating and knew she was trying to manage her feelings through food. Her friendships were with people she described as "having lots of drama going on in their lives." Lisa re-created, as an adult, the childhood relationships she had with her mother and father. She stayed in the background so as not to be a burden, and surrounded herself with versions of her father's alcoholic energy. Her body continued to hold on to the old family neglect through the tension she carried in her shoulders.

If you take a good look around at the people you have in your life, you will probably start to notice some family traits hidden there. Perhaps there are some folks who have the warmth of your mother, the negativity of your father, the sarcasm of your older brother, or the always-in-a-crisis needs of your younger sister. All the emotional qualities you grew up with, if distinct enough, become part of your emotional makeup. Whatever role you played in your family is often the role you will find yourself in with friends and coworkers. You may find yourself gravitating toward the toughest, most hard to please boss, because that is what your mother was like. You might find yourself trying to solve your coworkers' problems because that was your role in your alcoholic family.

Givers find takers, and vice versa. Because everyone else is carrying their own family influences, you will find that every bully finds his or her victim. Every leader will find those who have been taught to follow. This is an unconscious, unspoken energy that we put out toward each other, and we look for other "members" of our family to make us feel complete. That's why you can find yourself in relationships that initially feel familiar but end up feeling oppressive.

In my workshops, the subject of relationships brings up quite a bit of feelings. Questions about loyalty and support are explored and brought to the surface. When participants look at with whom they have chosen to spend time and why, they can be startled at the reasons. They believe they have people in their lives that matter to them, yet can be blind to who really is holding their best interests at heart. When they start to check in with how their bodies feel about their relationships, they begin to get clarity and answers.

WEEDING YOUR RELATIONSHIP GARDEN

How do you know who to keep, manage, or step away from when it comes to non-romantic relationships? You do it by raising your awareness of not only who you spend time with, but also how you want to be treated. As you start to look at the people around you, you will see how many of your interactions are based on habit and how many are based on a conscious choice. You will notice how your body feels around each person and what is required to keep the relationship going. For Linda and her former buddy, the amount of energy she was spending on her unsatisfying relationship was the turning point for her. She was not feeling the positive regard that is needed for healthy friendships, business relationships, and family ties.

What is positive regard? It is having the opinion or view about another person that includes a real belief in that person's innate goodness. You respect them, and they respect you. That does not mean the relationship will not require effort. No, it means that most of the time there is mutual consideration and respect when you interact. Those are the kinds of relationships you want to keep and cultivate more of in your life. If you tend to have interactions with others that take more and more of your energy, without any measure of enjoyment, it is time to take a second look.

FRIENDS IN NEED

Many words have been used to describe people who drain us. Julia Cameron, in her book *The Artist's Way*, describes the people who cause chaos in our lives as "crazy-makers." I use the phrase "main drains." Others have called them psychic vampires, leeches, and downers. You may have your own unique way of describing those people whom, after you spend time with them, make you feel badly about yourself or drained of energy. All these words seem to focus on energy: your energy and the energy of others. That is because we affect and are affected by the energy we put out into the world.

Have you ever had the experience of walking into a room and sensing from the people in it that something has happened? That something does not even have to be about you. It could be that bad news has been shared or that everyone on that particular Monday is having an "I don't want to be at work today" moment. We radiate messages through our energy, and that is how your best friend knows when to ask "what's wrong?" If you notice you are experiencing that kind of negative energy with most of the people with whom you spend time, it is time to start weeding your relationship garden.

We have only so much time and energy to give to others, and it is important to know how you are spending yours. Take a look at the quality of friendships, acquaintances, and groups in which you are involved by reviewing the next checklist.

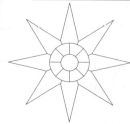

COMPASS POINTS
Social Connections Checklist

❀ Jot down in your journal or notebook the names of three to five people with whom you spend the most time in the following categories:

  ❀ Friendships:

  ❀ At work:

  ❀ Socially:

  ❀ On committees:

  ❀ School:

  ❀ Other Groups:

❀ What are some of the reasons you spend time with these people?

❀ How does your body's energy feel when you spend time with these individuals? Write a few words down next to each name. (Positive, drained, stimulated, challenged, picked on, supported.)

❀ If not a requirement, what would it feel like on a body level to let go of some of these relationships? (Relieved, happy, lonely, different.)

❀ If you do want to spend less time with "main drains," what is one step you can take this week?

If you generally feel positive with your friends and co-workers, that's great. If you don't, it's time to start looking at what old family dynamics you may be re-creating. What feels right because it is familiar may actually be wrong when it comes to your needs or sense of self today.

Say Goodbye to "Main Drains"

It is hard to say goodbye to relationships that served a purpose but no longer do. These are people whom you chose to be in your life, but the reason you did is now outdated. When you use your body's awareness you can decide whether you want to limit, or simply let go, of your contact with them. Some relationships, such as those of family, are permanent. But that does not mean you have to sacrifice your personality or self-esteem to make them work. Keep checking in with your body to see how you can tolerate these relationships, and then plan accordingly. You want to maintain a good relationship with yourself, and to do so you have to honor your needs and feelings.

If you do have to end a friendship because it is abusive, filled with drama, or no longer represents who you are today, you can choose to do so on your terms. Some of those endings will require a heartfelt, respectful conversation, and others require shutting the door and not being available. When those situations arise, ask your body and mind which method is best for you at this time. You cannot always avoid the pain of relationships ending, on either side, but you can take care of yourself to the best of your ability. Your inner voice will help you.

Friends in Deed

When Lisa started to examine with whom she was spending time and why, she realized she wanted to make changes. I wanted her to start noticing, in her body, when she felt the habitual need to get involved with dramatic people. As she did so, she shared with me how natural it felt for her to try and to fix things for other people. The role she had played in her family seemed to kick in automatically. That role was something she had adapted to as a child, but now it was time for something different.

I asked Lisa to name the qualities she wanted in her friendships, and it was hard for her to pinpoint them. I had her then describe the qualities that were the opposite of the dramatic and needy relationships in which she was usually involved. Lisa chose the words *calm, supportive*, and *positive*. I asked her if she could recognize that energy on a nonverbal level. She told me, "Yes, I can see it in how people carry themselves, the warmth in their eyes and how they are able to listen. When we checked in with her body's opinion, she felt lighter and less anxious. We then discussed ways Lisa could start cultivating new friendships that embodied more of what she wanted.

CULTIVATING THE NEW

When you want to make changes concerning with whom you spend time, it's important to choose the qualities you like and then turn your body compass toward finding them. Use the power of observation from both your body and mind when you meet new people. Watch how they express their personalities. Is it through the clothes they wear, the books they read, and the activities they pursue? All that information can be perceived if you allow yourself to be open to it. Listen to different discussions on movies, concerts, and food, and see if you want to join in. If someone you have met has a book, magazine, or piece of jewelry that looks interesting, ask him about it. Most folks like sharing information about things that have meaning to them. Cultivating your curiosity and using your body compass will help you discover all kinds of fascinating aspects about people and their interests.

Another way to invite new relationships into your life is to look at your daily routines. If your planned activities are feeling stale, it may be time to shake things up. What would it feel like to try something different and engage in activities about which you are curious? You will meet people that share your interests, and you have the potential to feel happier and more fulfilled. Ask your body how it feels about changing your routines and viewing a new landscape. If you get a definitive vote for change, take a look at the following exercise.

COMPASS POINTS
EXERCISE: WHAT'S NEW?

1. Close your eyes, and take a few deep inhales and exhales. Let yourself sit quietly.

2. Imagine the people with whom you like to spend time.

3. What are the qualities that draw you? (You can always look back at the **Social Connections Checklist** for some of the words you chose.) Write down those qualities. For example: Upbeat, social, into fitness, humor.

4. How does your body feel when you picture yourself spending time with those individuals?

5. If you don't have any of the relationships now, take a moment to list some of the things you enjoy. For example: Listening to music, hiking, painting, baseball.

6. Are any of those activities part of your life now?

7. If so, is there anyone you have met that you would like to get to know better?

8. What action could you take to create that interaction?

9. How does your body feel about taking that step? (Nervous, excited, shy.)

10. If those activities are not part of your life now, are you willing to try one of them in the near future?

11. What's one step you are willing to take this week toward exploring something new?

When you try new things and create new relationships, don't forget to appreciate who you are. Be true to yourself and value all the unique aspects of your personality and your tastes. If you enjoy classical music, art, sports, or writing, and want to explore those activities, let yourself do so. If you try something new and it turns out not to be your cup of tea, then at least you tried it. You don't have to give up who you are to have new experiences in your life

WHO YOU GONNA CALL?

Raising your body-mind awareness in regard to who supports you will be a powerful gift to yourself. Learning to recognize and rely on those who are truly there for you provides you with resources to keep going in all areas of your life. You will be able to distinguish true friends from "main drains" and free yourself from old roles. However, old habits can die hard, as was the case with Sandy.

Sandy had recently decided to change her high-power banking job and go back to school full-time to get a graduate degree in nutrition. She was both wildly excited and scared to make this change, but had longed to do so for the past two years. She had experienced many of the career signals I talked about in Week Three. She was getting strong body messages that she needed to shift her professional focus. Her stomach was jittery, she had chronic neck tension, and was feeling bored in her position at work.

Unfortunately, Sandy's mother was not too keen on her changing her career. She told Sandy about how hard it was to find a good job, and that leaving her present position was impulsive. There were many phone calls between the two, and Sandy often felt like she was on the witness stand defending her own life. Yet she was determined to go to school, and finally received an acceptance letter from a well-known college. She had a surprising reaction when she received the good news, and she shared it with me.

"You know, my first impulse, the day I got accepted to school, was to call my mother and tell her. I guess I was hoping for different response. I stopped myself, because I knew if I told her about my acceptance, she would not have been supportive. The rest of my conversation would have been me trying to convince her again about my choice. But, I almost did it anyway. I was so surprised at how tempted I was to still call her!"

NAYSAYERS

It is and is not surprising to whom we want to turn when thing are going well. Sometimes we turn to those who will celebrate with us, and other times we turn to those who will be critical. Although it seems odd that we would call someone who is potentially critical, it shows us how old emotional habits come into play. We turn to naysayers in order to keep our own pleasure contained and to keep our excitement down about our accomplishments. We turn to them because we wish those closest to us would finally give us what we have always wanted: their approval. But it is often the same negative response, and one of the most debilitating things we can do to ourselves.

The people who respond negatively to our personal and professional successes are usually afraid, and have suffered disappointments. They have not taken the risks they have wanted to and do not know how to handle pleasure, ambition, or expansion. This is good to know, but do not let it lull you into sharing new things if those individuals are not going to be supportive. Be discerning about to whom you reveal your dreams.

This next exercise will help your heart and head work together so you can select the best choices for your support system.

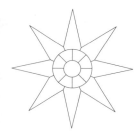

COMPASS POINTS
Exercise: Support System

1. Find a comfortable place to sit, on the floor, in a chair, or on a couch.
2. Close your eyes and focus on your breathing and your body.
3. Let your breathing return to the way you normally inhale and exhale.

4. Think of three to five people in your life whom you consider to be part of your support system or team. If there are more, that's great. (Remember, the most important criteria for making it on your list is that the person is 100-percent in your corner).

5. As you picture each person, think of what that person's strengths are. For example, good listener, empathetic, knows business, can make me laugh, can talk me down from the ceiling.

6. As you focus on each name and what that person's strengths are, pay attention to how your body feels. (Uplifted, buoyant, inspired, warm.)

7. Open your eyes and use this chart to write down the information you got.

   For Example:

Person	Strengths	How Your Body Feels
Pam	Business smarts	Calm, inspired

Once you have created your list, you can fine-tune the process by asking yourself what you may need now or in the future. This helps you choose the best person for support when the need arises.

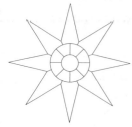

COMPASS POINTS
WHAT TO ASK FOR CHECKLIST

* Do I need to talk?
* Do I need to release emotion?
* Do I need advice?
* Do I need specific information?
* Do I just need to vent?
* Do I need a reality check?
* Do I need to be inspired?
* Do I need a cheerleader?
* Do I need to share successes?
* Do I need to share disappointment?
* Who from my list is best suited for what I need right now?

PROFESSIONAL POWER

Besides friendships, the people we hang out with professionally are vital to our success. The men and women with whom we work or network can be a great resource when we are pursuing professional goals. We need to pay attention to how we feel when we are with our professional colleagues. Who we envy, get inspired by, or get support from can influence the progression of our careers. If you find yourself stuck in some familial roles in your work environment, it would be wise to take stock. Do you spend time with colleagues who are positive about their lives, or those who appear to be invested in negativity?

Emily, a successful travel agent, found herself with a "main drain" dilemma. She shared her office space with a group of other agents, and, in time, formed friendly work relationships. The office group often had lunch and drinks together, and for a while it was comfortable. But in time, as Emily's career started to grow, she found herself reluctant to join the group at lunch or outside of work. Her lower back felt stiff and sore every time she left one of their gatherings. When she checked with her body to see what the back pain was about, she discovered that the group used the gatherings to trash the company, and it was draining to listen to. We all need to vent about work from time to time to keep things in perspective, but it can be wearing if that is only topic of discussion. Emily did not share the views of the group and was actually feeling positive about her job. After exploring what her body was telling her, Emily decided to reduce the amount of time she spent with her colleagues. She did not have to stop spending time with them completely; she just needed to balance the encounters with outside friends who shared her mindset. When she did so, she found that her body felt lighter and more relaxed when she was at work.

We do not have to make black-and-white, all-or-nothing decisions regarding those with whom we spend time professionally; we spend quite a bit of time our jobs and do not always have the luxury of choosing our coworkers. Some of us are in solitary careers without a lot of contact with others. In either scenario, what we are looking for is more balance. We want to notice how we feel when we spend time with others and ask our inner voice if we need a different infusion of professional energy.

Whether it is an association, club, or informal gathering of your own making, spending time with likeminded professionals is an energy-booster. These settings are the ones that provide companionship and stimulation. I belong to a local Toastmasters Club, and no matter the level of fatigue I may be feeling that day, after I leave a club meeting I feel revitalized. I know other colleagues who participate in a variety of organizations, and they do so not only for the business connections but also for the camaraderie. They want to be with people who share similar visions and help each other expand their careers. The gauge of whether the individuals or organization is the right fit is how your body feels during and after the time spent. When you seed your professional path with those who contribute to and share your growth, you create a powerful foundation for success.

The following exercise will help you gain perspective on your professional relationships now and for the future.

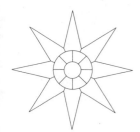

COMPASS POINTS
Exercise: Professional Pals

1. Sit quietly and take a few deep inhales and exhales.
2. Picture yourself in your professional environment.
3. Who are the people with whom you spend time in your workplace?

4. What words come to mind when you focus on each name?

5. What do you notice in your body when you read those words?

6. Is there anyone you would like to get to know better?

7. What one step can you take this week to make that happen?

8. Are there any organizations, clubs, or associations you have thought about exploring?

9. Are there people with whom you would like to form an informal group?

10. What's one action you can take toward that goal?

11. How does your body feel about taking the step?

12. Write down your answers in your notebook or journal.

COMMUNITY

Besides your personal friends and professional colleagues, there are others who cross our path on a daily basis. Whether you live in a small town or a big city, having connections to the people in your neighborhood helps you build a sense of community. These are the folks you see while walking your dog, on your commute, or when going to the dry cleaners. The ones who belong to your church, gym, or PTA. I have noticed that, when I take the time to greet people, even if it's only once, I feel more a part of my community. It helps me realize that I am an individual among many, and that we all share this world. When there was a blackout in New York City a few years ago, it was our neighbors and local

shop and restaurant owners who rallied and supported each
other. Many of our friends were stranded on opposite ends
of town. If you are feeling lonely, take the time to connect
in a small way to the people in your world to help you feel
less isolated. Julie found it liberating.

A high-powered attorney, Julie found herself working
long hours at a new firm in a new city. Although she enjoyed her work, she found herself feeling lonely. Though
she tried to make time for friends and networking, she found
herself too tired to follow up. Her upper back felt tense,
and she also often felt tension in her forehead. She complained to me that her new city was unfriendly and harsh.

Julie asked me if she was creating an inaccurate picture,
and, if so, how she could change her perspective. I asked
her if she was open to trying an experiment in community-
building. She was willing, so I assigned her this homework
for the next two weeks: Every person she ran into, whether
it was her bus driver or neighbor, she was to either smile at
or say hello. Julie already had a sense in her body of what
felt good or bad and could gauge positive energy. She was
to let go the importance of whether someone said hello
back and just concentrate on making contact.

After the two weeks, Julie reported that she felt a difference. She discovered that her city was filled with people
who were actually friendly. They might not end up being
her closest companions, but they did make up the fabric of
her community. Even if she simply discussed the weather
with a neighbor in the elevator, there was opportunity to
relate to people. In time and through small interactions,
Julie found out many interesting things about her new area.
This allowed her to feel more at ease. She continued to greet

people who crossed her path and felt her small effort give back big returns.

This chapter has looked at the connections we make with others throughout our lives. Your body's response will provide the clues you need to get the best support. Whether you are in personal or professional relationships, you want to feel that you are experiencing mutual positive regard. Though the imprint of childhood may cause you to seek out old roles, your inner voice will help you define new ones.

COMPASS POINTS
WEEK FOUR ASSIGNMENTS

1. Continue with the **Four-Part Breathing** exercise. What are you noticing about how your body feels when you do this exercise?

2. Continue with the **What Does My Body Need?** exercise and now try it at different points in the day. Try and use it when you are choosing what foods to eat, music you want to listen to, and what to do for relaxation.

3. What people bring you the most support, wisdom, and joy? Create the time to be with them even if it's over the phone.

4. Where are you spending your time and energy? If you do have to interact with people who are not necessarily in your corner, who can you call to ask for support? Think of all the people you can

contact either in the moment or in advance when you need an ally. Use your **Support System Checklist**.

5. What activities do you *want* to participate in, and what activities do you *have* to participate in? Start noticing the difference and make sure there is good balance between the two. Continue to monitor where you want to put your energy. Use your body as a gauge to see if you feel anxious or calm when accepting an invitation.

6. Try the community-building homework in this chapter and make an effort to connect with others in your community. Take note of how your body and mind respond to your effort.

(((((((((CHAPTER SIX)))))))))

Week Five:
Relationship Central

We can only learn to love by loving.

—Iris Murdoch

"I knew by our second date that he wasn't the right guy for me. I should have paid attention." Terry's face was sad and she spoke in a soft voice as she told me her story. I asked what she meant, and she said, "I had this feeling in my chest, I almost can't explain it, but it was when I asked him if he could get my coat from the other room. He said in a very sharp voice for me to *get it myself,* like he was angry. When I asked him if he was serious, he said no, he was only kidding. But, you know something, he wasn't, and that was his pattern, not telling me the truth and hiding who he was. Here I am, six months later, and he's disappeared."

Terry had an instinct about her now ex-boyfriend and it turned out she was right. She ignored the warning signs, and it caused her quite a bit of heartache. In this chapter, you will look at how you can tell who is right for you, by tuning in to your body's response. Now, this can be a little tricky because there's often a battle between what your body feels and what your heart feels. We're talking desire versus true love. Although attraction is very much a part of being in love, you don't want it to be the *only* thing holding your relationships together. So, even though there's a mix of both in romantic relationships, you still want to use your body-mind connection to figure out who's a good match. What it will come down to is how you want to be treated and how you ultimately feel with the person you have chosen. You want to know you matter, not only to another person, but also to yourself.

THE RIGHT STUFF

There is much that happens when we fall for someone: the body responds, the mind responds, and there is often a rush of energy within us. In fact, it's fairly common for people to describe love as a sensation of "being swept away," that what's happening to them goes against all rational thought and logic. This roller-coaster ride can be filled with feelings of happiness and joy, or a journey that is fraught with drama, pain, and self-neglect.

Susan was a bright, sweet, and caring young woman. She loved people and was known for her kindness and sensitivity. Always tuned into the needs of others, she often forgot what she was feeling and needing for herself. Susan was involved with a man whom she felt she loved, but she also had some reservations. She shared with me that her boyfriend was strong, focused on his career, and valued strength in others. I asked what mattered to her in romantic relationships. Susan mentioned that she wanted to feel that she was viewed as intelligent, and then shyly added that she loved romantic gestures. When I asked if her current boyfriend viewed her as intelligent, she hesitated and said "I guess so." When I checked in on the romantic gestures part, she said, "Well, he's really focused on his career and feels that creating a strong financial foundation is what is most important in life. There's something exciting about being with him. I feel like I have to be on my best behavior." I thought these were interesting qualities for Susan to report on, because she hadn't yet mentioned how this relationship satisfied what mattered to her.

When we asked for the opinion of Susan's body toward this relationship, she said she sometimes felt tense when she was with her boyfriend, "A bit nervous in my stomach and tight in my shoulders." We explored what those body signals meant, and Susan said, "I guess it's because I feel I never know where I stand with him. Sometimes he's affectionate, but most times he's not. He is such a powerful guy, and I get a thrill when I think of that." Of all the things Susan described I hadn't heard one of her emotional needs mentioned. Something was off in this picture.

There is a common misconception in romantic relationships that the feeling of being "swept off your feet" or being "off balance" is an intuitive sign the person is right for you. Actually, it is not. Attraction alone does not always mean the person is suitable for us (later in the book we will look at how family history and emotional habits influence who we have in our lives). What *does* matter is a sense of connection and trust. I know that doesn't sound very romantic, but believe me, I'm not negating romance and chemistry. I'm a big fan of both, and they are very important in establishing relationships. What I'm referring to are the qualities that allow relationships to endure and evolve, those shared beliefs and ideals that create our romantic partnerships and keep them going. Who we think we want in our lives and who actually is the better fit is an interesting issue to explore.

ILLUSION VS. REALITY

For a few years, Diane had been telling me she wanted a *real* relationship. So how come she kept dating a variety of men who readily admitted they were not ready for any kind of relationship? Well, according to Diane, these men were fun, spontaneous, and didn't expect anything from her. There seemed to be no pressure, except Diane was experiencing a growing stress around scheduling dates and having her dates commit to times they could meet. She admitted there was something exhilarating about not knowing when they were going to call, kind of exciting and intense, but it was ultimately a letdown when she did not hear from them. That's when being spur-of-the-moment wasn't so enjoyable for Diane. When she looked at her choices, she realized that dating these free spirits only provided her with the *illusion* of romance.

Diane both feared and desired a committed relationship. An only child, she had witnessed infidelity with her parents and had seen the heartbreak they caused each other. This difficult background made her distrustful of men, and she chose the ones to whom she never had to give her heart. But the heart has a mind of its own, and Diane's held a strong need to love. Even though she tried to convince herself she wanted things to be light, her chest felt hollow when she came home to an empty apartment. She thought she was getting what she wanted, but realized that what she really wanted was to break her pattern.

THE COOKIE OR THE REAL MEAL

Diane was into health and fitness, so I asked her to look at her dating style as if she were choosing her next meal. I asked her to consider what her body craved when she was really hungry and to go with whatever came to mind first, when she needed food fast. For Diane, it was cookies, especially sugar cookies. She told me, "Nothing seems to taste as good as those cookies when I just can't wait any longer." I asked her to remember how her body feels after she has those cookies. She said, "Really energized, and then I crash and feel like I can't move." I reminded her that waiting too long to eat causes us to grab the most convenient food we can—a quick fix. Ultimately those fast feasts aren't really satisfying when your body needs a good, nourishing meal. I wanted to know what Diane's ideal meal was, and it came to her right away. She said quickly, "Homemade lasagna. You know the kind, as it comes out of the oven with the cheese melting on those layers of pasta and tomato sauce?" I could really picture it from her description!

I asked Diane to apply the cookie or lasagna standard, when she was deciding on her next dates. She was to ask her body whether the man she was going out with was a sugar cookie or a dish of that sumptuous, homemade lasagna. This comparison would allow her to know exactly what she was getting if she chose to continue to date a guy she was interested in. In doing so, she was checking in to see if the man she was seeing was capable of giving her what she wanted. Could she connect to him emotionally, or was he just a delicious, sweet treat? Remember, choosing cookies is not about being bad or good. If that is you want, go for it. But if not, cookies will never satisfy you the way your favorite meal will.

TOP PRIORITY

We all have our own definition of what true love is to us. Yet there are some universal themes that define successful romantic relationships. Judith Wallerstein, who studied marriages in her book *The Good Marriage*, noted that successful relationships were built on a foundation of respect and a sense each person had of being cherished by the other. What seems to matter was that each person felt he or she was a top priority with his or her partner.

In my work with couples, it's always interesting to hear people describe, in body terms, whether they have that sense of being a top priority. Without asking them to use their bodies as a gauge, they will describe the quality of their relationship with phrases such as, "it's a feeling I have inside," "a trust I have in my gut," or "an emptiness in my heart." Without consciously being aware they're doing it, their bodies are brought into the dialog.

We all have our own innate sense of what it feels like to be cherished or special. For one person it might be the giving and receiving of affection such as holding hands or being hugged. For another, feeling as though she is a top priority means that all the bills are paid on time, and for others it may mean getting a daily call to say hello. Most times the feeling of knowing we matter is a tangible feeling of security, deep within our bodies.

RESPECT

Another important aspect in relationships, respect, means that you accept your romantic partner for who he or she is. You respect his right to feel what he feels, believe what he believes, and evolve as person at his own pace. I'm sure you've met people who said, "I just knew she was the one." And when you ask them how they knew, they say, "It felt right." They use words and phrases to explain the emotions that they feel, such as "I felt calm, serene, complete, comfortable, in sync." These words describe what you feel inside when you meet someone who just clicks with you. It doesn't mean that there is not excitement, mystery, or those wonderful highs when we first fall in love. What it does mean is that there is a sense deep inside of us that this person is not someone who creates feelings of anxiety, cautiousness, or despair when we are with them. We are respected, and there is a sense of security. But what causes a sense of security within the body?

Security comes from knowing that the way a person represents himself to you is actually who he is; the confidence that comes from knowing that when someone tells you she will be faithful, true to her word, and present in the relationship, then that is how she will be. It's not a matter of expecting perfection from another person; it's a matter of knowing that the person you love is someone on whom you can have healthy dependence.

Healthy dependence occurs when you believe and know, from concrete experience, that the person you are involved with will behave in a trustworthy manner a majority of the time. It's not to be confused with codependency, which is the giving-up of your sense of self for the needs of another person. Healthy dependency provides us with the inner knowledge that someone else respects—and yes, loves—us enough to honor our needs. They keep their word to the best of their ability, and we keep ours with them.

RELATIONSHIP BLOCKERS

When our romantic relationships are in balance, we know it. Whether it's new or long-term, we are relaxed with our partner and have a sense of ease. When things are not in harmony, that effortless way of relating quickly flies away. You become uneasy, and perceive, in your body and mind, the distance between you. Many times your perceptions are accurate, and you try to find ways to bridge the emotional gap. These are normal glitches that happen with all couples. However, if you and your partner are in constant conflict, or have a long-standing distance, it needs exploring. Either some fundamental values are not in sync, or you are running into relationship stumbling blocks of which you may not be aware.

I have noticed some common triggers that cause tension and conflict with many couples. If you are currently in a relationship that initially felt right but now feels wrong, it's time to check in on these relationship-blockers. Here are four behaviors that cause communication breakdown in romantic partnerships.

Projection

Projections are negative beliefs you have about yourself that you place upon another person. Then you act toward that person as if he was *feeling those things about you.* Let's say you were feeling insecure about a dinner you were planning for your extended family. You doubt your cooking skills, you worry about the dishes you have chosen, and generally think the worst about your ability to pull it off. Then your significant other innocently asks how the dinner menu is coming along. The next thing you know, you are accusing her of criticizing you or judging you for not having the meal perfectly planned. This is a projection in action.

To discover a projection, notice how strongly you respond to a straightforward question or statement. If you find you having an intense reaction, stop and get a grip. Take a moment to get a *reality check* by asking the other person what he means by the question or statement. This usually clarifies the situation.

If you feel you are on the receiving end of a projection, say you don't understand what's going on. Be sure to follow up by saying you want to understand and are willing to listen. If it's too confusing for you to figure out your loved one's strong response, take a break and address it later when you both are calmer. Check in to see if the other person was aware of her strong reaction, and ask her to help you figure out how you both can handle it in the future.

Broken Promises

One of the biggest ways to break trust with someone you love is to tell him you will do something, and then not do it. When you make an agreement with another person and then do not do what you promised, you create hurt feelings and mistrust. It's important to take responsibility for breaking a promise and take immediate action to rectify the situation. If there is a pattern of breaking agreements either by you or by the other person, then the reasons for that pattern have to be explored. Sometimes we say yes to avoid conflict, and sometimes we take on more than we realize and don't ask for help when necessary. Before you make a promise to your loved one, check to see that you are willing and able to complete what you agreed to. If you decide to commit, make your best effort to follow through.

Unexpressed Needs

Feelings or needs about a person or situation that don't get expressed are big relationship-blockers. If you don't tell others what you need from them, for whatever reason, it inevitably backfires. Emotions don't go away, and if they are not expressed directly, they get expressed indirectly through behaviors such as sulking, teasing, or complaining about everything except what is really bothering you. Unexpressed feelings also show as physical symptoms, ranging from headaches to ulcers to teeth-grinding. These painful physical signals show the effort the body has to go through to manage unexpressed emotions.

We can't control the outcome when we express our needs, because there is usually someone else who has needs as well. However, it's better to express what you want or don't want right from the beginning. You can always negotiate getting your needs met from there.

Unrealistic Expectations

An unrealistic expectation is when you want another person to fulfill the parts of you or your life that are your responsibility. Your partner cannot nor is required to fill areas in your life that are blocked or stuck. Partners can inspire, support, and challenge you, but ultimately you are an individual within a relationship and need to be responsible for your own creative, spiritual, or career happiness.

In turn, you cannot fix someone, solve their problems, or get them to do something that they are not ready to do or simply doesn't want to do. However, if the mood of the person who is stuck affects your relationship in a negative way, you can address that issue by expressing how it makes y o u feel and asking for her help in the solution.

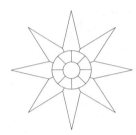

COMPASS POINTS

RELATIONSHIP BLOCKER CHECKLIST

❈ Do you feel you are a priority to your partner?

❈ How does your body feel about it?

❈ Do you feel respected in the relationship?

❈ What does your body tell you?

❈ Are you aware of any negative beliefs about you or your partner that you may be projecting onto each other?

❈ What are they?

❈ How does your body feel when you read the list?

❈ Have there been any promises or agreements you have made with your loved one that you have not honored?

❈ Name the most important.

❈ Have you been disappointed or hurt by any promises made to you that have been broken?

❈ What is the most important one?

❈ What do feel in your body when you name that broken promise?

❀ Is there something you need or want from your partner that you haven't expressed to him or her?

❀ What is that need?

❀ How does it feel in your body to not express what you need?

❀ Have you been expecting your significant other to fill in any areas of your life that are actually your responsibility?

❀ What are those areas?

❀ If you have identified some areas with blocks, are you willing to make any changes?

❀ Name the most important area.

❀ What is the first step you are willing to take this week?

❀ How does your body feel when you imagine taking that step?

DARTS TO THE HEART

Besides relationship-blockers, there is another series of actions we possibly do to our loved ones that can cause emotional damage. These *darts to the heart* are tactics used in relationships that are hurtful and unfair. If you are on the receiving end of these behaviors, they feel terrible. If you use them against your partner, the bond of love and affection between you will deteriorate. Most darts to the heart show up during conflicts, but I have also seen them used simply to provoke another person. Take a look at these lethal darts to the heart and see if they are part of how you behave in your relationship.

Fearsome Fury

When fearsome fury, otherwise known as rage, is the common reaction by you or your significant other, you are engaging in a destructive form of communication. Rage is an accumulation of unexpressed emotions ranging from hurt to fear to anger. Rage can show up as full-blown screaming, and is often at the root of some of the other darts I will mention. When it's full-out, it is scary to witness and scary to receive. In this form, it can be physically felt by another person, and creates wariness and distrust. Rage should never be tolerated, and when it happens, whomever it's being aimed at should get out of the line of fire. Having a rational discussion at that point is useless. Only afterward can a real conversation about the impact of rage occur.

Sarcastic Slam

Sarcasm is an indirect expression of anger and hurt. When you use sarcasm toward people, you are trying in a deliberate manner to shame and demean them. You are basically letting another person know that his emotions are unacceptable to you, because you feel you are superior in some way. This is a dart that stops healthy communication in its tracks.

If you find yourself on the receiving end of sarcasm, do not try to continue your discussion or argument. Let the other person know you will speak with her when she is ready to listen. When that level of contempt enters a relationship, on a consistent basis, it has to be addressed and not tolerated. Later on in this chapter, I will discuss ways to approach those conversations.

Cold Shoulder

Withdrawal, known as the "cold shoulder," is another indirect method of conveying hurt and anger. When you or another person withdraws from your relationship, you are breaking the connection with each other. It's like being a kid and taking all your toys home because you can't have your way. Most people emotionally withdraw because they are overwhelmed and scared by what they are feeling. They act defensively and pull inward to protect themselves. Doing so leaves the other feeling helpless until you decide you are ready to talk again. You end up punishing your significant other in a nonverbal manner. Even if your reasons for being hurt are valid, it is still unfair to shut someone out.

If you are with someone who withdraws, tell him you will be happy to speak with him when he is ready. You will let him know you will not keep trying to resolve the problem if he continues to reject you. After you've communicated that, be friendly and loving, but not a doormat.

Dismissed

Imagine telling someone how you feel and having her turn around and say, "You don't know what you're talking about," or "That's ridiculous." Even as I write these words, I feel my own body cringe when I picture myself hearing them. When you dismiss someone else's reaction you are basically rejecting the person. Similar to sarcasm, you negate the other person's right to feel what he feels. This a form of control; the person doing the dismissing controls which emotions are acceptable and which aren't. When you are dismissed by your significant other, you no longer have equal partnership. And if you are the one doing the dismissing, you will eventually create an atmosphere of fear.

Counter-Punch

We've all had this experience: We are accused of not doing something, such as washing the dishes, and the next thing we know we are battling back with our own set of complaints such as, "Well you didn't call me when you said you would and you never make the bed!" All of sudden we are in a tennis match, with so many verbal volleys that the original upset gets lost.

If counter-punching or -attacking is your style, you will find yourself in endless arguments that don't get resolved. Whether it is you or the other person who wants to be heard, being met with a counterattack will keep you both on a hamster wheel of arguing. The best way to jump off is to hear out the other person before you respond. It's hard to do, but will stop you from upping the ante and help you understand why you each may be hurt.

Negative Name Game

In the heat of an argument, we aren't always able to rein in what we say. Our body is in battle-station mode, and we can end up saying irrational and hurtful things to our partner. That's when negative name-calling can show up in a heated discussion. Name-calling did not feel good in second grade, and it does not feel any better today. When you use it, you verbally go after someone's vulnerable spots, and when we are angry, we often know where to poke our sharp sticks.

Name-calling affects self-esteem, and if you use it as a tactic, you are attacking your loved one's sense of self. If you are on the receiving end, do not try to top the other person by throwing names back. Instead, give her one warning that you need her to stop, and then take a break until she has calmed down.

Fountain of Tears

Hearing that tears are a dart to the heart may initially ruffle a few feathers. Let me say upfront that I am not suggesting that we can't or shouldn't cry. Tears are a very important form of emotional expression and release. However, they become darts to the heart when they are used to manipulate someone or stop an important conversation. If *every* time we are challenged or confronted we collapse and cry, the other person has to shift attention from his needs to ours. He ends up taking care of us instead of being heard. In time this causes resentment and frustration to build.

If most of your arguments end with someone crying and another person feeling guilty, then something is out of balance in the communication. It hurts not to be heard, and just because someone doesn't cry as easily doesn't mean she is not in pain.

Take a look at the following list of words. Notice and describe, without over-thinking, how your body feels when you imagine being on the receiving end of them.

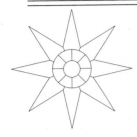

COMPASS POINTS
Darts to the Heart Checklist

Dart	Body Reaction
Fearsome Fury	
Sarcastic Slam	
Cold Shoulder	
Dismissed	
Counter-Punch	
Negative Name Game	
Fountain of Tears	

Relationship Builders

We've looked at the actions that cause turbulence in relationships and the effect they have on your body. Now let's focus on finding the tools you can use to get your relationship back on track.

Bill and Terry were newly married and deeply in love, but living together as if they were still two single people. Despite a great deal of compatibility, they found themselves in the same argument loop. Their main relationship-blocker was unexpressed need. They tended not to consult with each other on plans or directly ask for what they wanted in terms of time and attention. Consequently, they always felt disappointed, because the other person could not read their minds. The result of them not expressing their emotional needs was ongoing fights with the main *dart to the heart* being the counter-punch.

The first tool we worked with together was having Bill and Terry listen to each other when one person was upset. Listening and expressing your understanding of the issue being presented is one of the most effective ways to keep arguments from escalating. Remember how you have felt when you sensed that someone understood you. I've watched fighting couples visibly relax when they perceive that they had their partner's attention and understanding. Bill and Terry practiced this technique every time one of them had something to say, and refrained from counter-attacking. This created trust between them, which allowed them to express their other needs more directly. In the end, they became more united as a couple while maintaining their individuality.

TOOLS FOR RELATIONSHIP-BUILDING AND CONFLICT RESOLUTION

 **COMPASS POINTS**

When your significant other confronts or addresses you about a specific issue, take a deep breath and:

- ❀ **Listen:** Place your attention on the other person; don't interrupt.

- ❀ **Ask questions:** Ask the person to explain why she is upset because "I really want to know and understand." Then when she tells you, listen.

- ❀ **Apologize:** Tell her you're sorry you hurt her: "I get that I really hurt you and I'm sorry about that." (Even if it was unintentional on your side or a total misunderstanding, apologize. You can always talk about the misunderstanding later.) Tell her that you understand her hurt. For example, "I'm sorry. I see how not listening was hurtful."

After you've had this discussion, use your body as a gauge to determine if you feel relaxed. If you do, that's a sign you are back in sync. If not, there may be something you need to express or follow up with. When you are the one who is upset or needs to bring up an issue, try the following techniques.

COMPASS POINTS

- ❀ **Calm down:** Get yourself into as calm a state as possible. Do the **Calm Down** breathing exercise from Week Two and get in touch with what's really bothering you. You don't have to cut off your feelings; you just don't want to be out of control.
- ❀ **Use "I" language:** State your feelings from an "I" place. "I feel [x] when you say or do [y]. I need [x] from you because I feel [y] when you act that way."
- ❀ **Allow for answers:** Once you have stated your feelings, give the other person time to respond. You can always ask questions if anything remains unclear.

After you have told your partner what's bothering you, check in with your body to see if you feel calm. If not, use the **What Does My Body Need?** exercise from Week One, to see what you may need from your partner.

If you find you are both too upset to resolve your discussion, plan a separate conversation that occurs when you are feeling calm. This is called a preliminary conversation, and occurs before any future conflicts.

COMPASS POINTS

❈ **Preliminary conversation:** Have a conversation when you are not in the heat of battle about what each of you needs from the other.

   For example:

   ❈ "We seem to be fighting a lot about money, and I want to figure out a way to talk about it so that we both don't feel attacked."

   ❈ "I could use your help in coming up with solution on how we can communicate better."

   You also may want to choose a place that feels neutral, such as such as your kitchen, the park, or backyard to have this conversation.

❈ **Feeling overwhelmed:** If you are having an argument and you need to take a break, tell the other person so, and that you want to come back to the discussion later because the issue—and he—is important to you.

❀ When you are taking an emotional break, check in with yourself:

    ❀ Ask yourself what this fight is really about. Is it about the dishes, messiness, or chronic lateness, or is it really about the impact of those issues on you or the other person? Get to the heart of the matter.

    ❀ Ask yourself if you have brought any of your own stuff into the argument. Have your mood or unexpressed needs contributed to the conflict?

Arguments, misunderstandings, and hurt feelings are all part of relationships, but they shouldn't be happening a majority of the time. If they are, seek out some form of professional guidance. The greatest gift you can give to your significant other is not having to win every argument. The real prize is having someone in your life with whom you can share your heart. If you tune in to your own needs and find ways to express them, you will have better communication. So what's your style of communication?

VERBAL OR ACTION-ORIENTED

How we express our care for our partners may not be the same way they communicate with us. When it comes to emotional styles of expression, some people are verbal, and others are action-oriented. A verbal style means that words of affection and acknowledgment register as love. The person hearing them physically relaxes, responds emotionally, and feels reassured. This style means asking how their day was, telling them you love them, or giving them compliments.

An action-oriented style of emotional communication shows people you love them by *doing*. It's a nonverbal demonstration of care that can be missed. I have worked with couples such that one person complains that she doesn't feel loved, and the other one says something such as, "But I handle all our finances and make sure I'm home every night for dinner." The person who is action-oriented feels he is showing his care through his deeds, and often expects the same kind of behavior. The same idea goes for the verbal person.

How *you* express yourself emotionally is usually how you like to receive emotions. This holds true for your husband, wife, girlfriend, or boyfriend. What one person thinks is being expressed as love may not make an impression because the other person has a different system. Using words registers as affection for one, and taking action registers as love for the other.

What do you do when you have people with two different styles of emotional expression? You find out what works for them and try to give that to them most of the time. Just because your style fits you, doesn't mean it does for your partner.

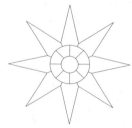

COMPASS POINTS
STYLES OF COMMUNICATION CHECKLIST

✿   How do I best express my emotional self? Verbally or in an action-oriented way?

❀ How does my partner express his or her emotional self? Verbally or in an action-oriented way?

❀ Does my partner need me to express my emotional self in a different way? (You don't have to give up your style, but you can also give your partner more of what registers as love and care to him or her. You will both benefit.)

❀ What do I need from my partner in order to feel that I am loved and cared for? (Tell your partner what registers with you.)

❀ When I think of giving my significant other what he or she needs in order to feel loved, what do I feel in my body?

❀ How does my body feel when I imagine receiving expressions of love in the way that matches me?

TRUE TO YOU

In order to sustain or invite a great romantic partnership in your life, you need to identify the qualities in relationships that are important to you. The more you know yourself, the more you can find the best person for you. Your relationship with you becomes the blueprint for all others. What elements are vital to your happiness when it comes to romance? Even if you are already in a long-term relationship, it's good to revisit this question to see if you and your partner continue to share what is important.

You can do the next two exercises together or separately.

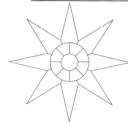

COMPASS POINTS

EXERCISE: BODY-MIND BOTTOM LINES

1. Sit comfortably, in a chair or on the floor, with your eyes closed.

2. Use the **Four-Part Breathing** exercise you learned in Week One.

3. Let your breathing return to normal.

4. Ask yourself: What qualities, values, and behaviors are important to me in a romantic relationship? (Humor, loyalty, love of children, love of animals, marriage, commitment, affection, ability to make money, artistic.)

5. Open your eyes.

6. Write down as many of them that come to mind.

7. After you have made your list, take a moment to look at each word.

8. Pause on each and ask yourself: If I had to give up this value, how would it feel?

9. Focus on both your body's and mind's reactions and write them down next to the word.

   For example: Affection

   > If I had to give up affection in a romantic relationship I would feel: Sad.
   > Body Feeing: My throat feels closed, and my chest feels tense.

10. When you have completed your list, take three or four deep breaths, in through your nose and out through your mouth.

You probably had some strong body reactions when you contemplated giving up the qualities that are significant to you. Again, it's a reminder that you have the body smarts to know when you are compromising yourself in relationships. The following exercise will also help you get in touch with anything you are dismissing in yourself.

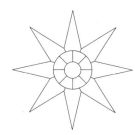

COMPASS POINTS

EXERCISE: BODY-MIND DEAL-BREAKERS

1. Sit comfortably with your eyes closed.
2. Do the **Four-Part Breathing** exercise.
3. Let your breathing return to normal.
4. Ask yourself: What behaviors or qualities would I not tolerate in a romantic relationship? (Smoking, inability to communicate, no desire for children, dislike of dogs, drug use, dislike of travel.)
5. Open your eyes and turn to your journal.
6. Write down as many as come to mind.
7. After you have made your list, take a moment to look at each word or phrase you have written.
8. Focus on each one and ask yourself, "If I had to tolerate these qualities or behaviors, what would my body and mind have to say? "

For Example: Not an animal lover.

       Mind: Angry.

       Body: Tightness in my shoulders.

In this chapter we looked at how we create and participate in romantic relationships. The more you listen to what your inner voice is expressing about love, the more you will be guided toward the best connection for you. Use the exercises in this chapter to help you figure out what matters to your heart.

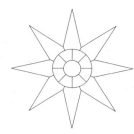

COMPASS POINTS

WEEK FIVE ASSIGNMENTS

1. Continue with the **Four-Part Breathing** and notice if your body is responding faster to the effects of the exercise.

2. Continue with the **What Does My Body Need?** exercise and try using it at different points during the day. Ask yourself if the questions are starting to feel natural and/or more comfortable.

3. If you are in a relationship, find out the emotional style of communication that registers with your partner as love.

4. Go back to the **Relationship Blocker Checklist** and see if you need to let your loved one know about any of your answers.

5. Check the **Darts to the Heart Checklist** and practice not using these darts when you are communicating.

6. If you are not in a relationship, write down all the qualities you want in one by using the **Body-Mind Bottom Lines** exercise in this chapter. Post this in a visible place in your home or keep it where you can read it daily.

(((((((((CHAPTER SEVEN)))))))))

Week Six:
Home Spaces and Workplaces

The ache for home lives in all of us, the safe place where we can go as we are and not be questioned.

—Maya Angelou

Jason, a New York City transplant, had wanted to move from his one-bedroom apartment for years but was stuck with a "but it's such a good rent" mentality. He lived in a fourth-floor walkup, and in time had watched his neighborhood transform into one he hardly recognized. What used to be an area known for its unique stores and specialty food shops had now become a place filled with large retails stores and generic-looking buildings. Despite the changes in his outside world, Jason's inside one wasn't budging. Every time he came home, he felt the same tiredness creep over his body, especially around his shoulders. "I have this blah feeling when I walk into my living room," he told me. "I've changed the furniture, painted the walls, and gotten new carpet. Despite all that, I still don't like where I'm living, and I know in my heart it's not where I want to be." Having a "good" rent was actually not so good for Jason, and he felt it daily.

When Jason talked about his unhappiness in a workshop, he said he feared moving, because he had no concept of where he wanted to go. The thought of making a drastic geographical move was keeping him paralyzed, which showed up as the weight he carried on his shoulders. For Jason, the drab but familiar home he was living in was more tolerable then the idea of moving. Even though his instinct was telling him that his apartment no longer fit, he could not take action. Finding where he wanted to live became his goal when he joined a Find Your Inner Voice Goals group. He wanted and needed to work with his body's signals to get him pointed in the right direction.

Early in his exploration, Jason got a very clear message from his inner voice about staying on the East Coast but residing in a smaller city such as Boston. He explained to me what he imagined he would like about living there. "When I picture myself in a small yet lively city, I get this excited feeling in my chest and stomach. The sensation is different from the fear I felt about moving." As the weeks continued, Jason described to the group how he saw himself walking around the streets of Boston. As he did so, a persistent image of an apartment kept coming to his mind. "I see one of those old-fashioned buildings with a large bay window that has some steps leading up to the door. It's located in a neighborhood that really feels like a neighborhood, and I have this warm sensation in my chest when I see myself sitting in the living room." He kept focusing on those positive sensations in his body, which helped him validate what he really wanted.

Jason eventually visited Boston and walked around the city in the way he had always pictured. About eight months after our group ended, he ended up relocating to Boston. I received a card from him telling me he was happy and doing well. What started out as dissatisfaction with an apartment actually became a move to another city, and Jason's instinct was the catalyst.

HOME MATTERS

Many of us don't give much thought to where we hang our hats at night, but "home" is one of the most important ingredients when it comes to the rejuvenation of our spirit. Home is our place for self-reflection and relaxation. If your home doesn't feel right, nothing else will. We all need that place where we can unwind and get comfortable. Our dwelling is where we recharge our batteries, dream our dreams, and care for ourselves and others.

Where we live and how we inhabit the space is something we must consider throughout our lives. The way we feel about ourselves is directly related to the way we set up our homes and offices. Even now, you may be uncomfortable or dissatisfied with your current place of residence and are looking to find answers for why it doesn't feel right. The solution can be as simple as repositioning your furniture, or as complex as an out-of-town move. What's your body telling you about where and how you live?

You will have the opportunity to explore and answer that question, using your body compass. Doing so will help you figure out and know whether you are living in the right place. If you are not where you want to be, you can discover some ways to find the right spot or make changes to where you already live. You will also have the chance to evaluate the quality of your life as it relates to the spaces in which you dwell. There is a connection between the two, and it not only affects your energy but also the energy of others.

HIDDEN MEANINGS

Barbara was seeing a new guy, whom she had felt really good about. He was funny, smart, and earned a living as a consultant. After dating a couple of weeks, everything seemed great, until Barbara got a glimpse of how her new boyfriend lived. "I walked into his house, and my stomach flipped. I was shocked at what I saw. There were newspapers and magazines piled up in the corners of his living room. He had an old-fashioned lamp with a beautiful glass shade in his hallway, yet there was an obvious crack running through it. And on top of that, the paint on the kitchen ceiling was peeling!" Barbara remembered thinking, "What is going on here? Maybe I should reconsider dating this guy."

What was interesting about this scenario was that Barbara's new man was not unaware of the problems in his home and expressed his embarrassment to her. His excuse was that he did not have the time for upkeep due to his hectic work schedule. But he had bought the house six years previously, and had not made any attempt to address the issues of clutter or repairs. What did Barbara think? Well, despite her initial reaction of shock, she started thinking, "This man makes a good living and probably has not had someone to help him fix up his place. I can be that person, because everything he says sounds reasonable."

Barbara ended giving her outwardly successful guy a chance even though her instinctive reaction was to back away. You may already have guessed the end to this story. Barbara's initial feeling ended up being very accurate. Her boyfriend's indifference to his apartment, where the space reflected a lack of commitment, ultimately showed up in their relationship. Barbara's offers and attempts to help him fix up his home were rebuffed. After dating for close to a year, Barbara's boyfriend ended the relationship, because he was not ready to "get serious." His attitude was reflected in the way he treated his home.

HOME STYLE

I know you have had the experience of walking into someone's home and picking up lots of information about him or her. The furniture, colors, art, or lack thereof, communicates quite a bit about who that person is. The message being sent can be one of self-acceptance, joy, and confidence, or it can be one that displays the inner unhappiness of the person living there. A home shows a lot about what's important to its inhabitants. My friend Rebecca's home overflows with games, puzzles, and stuffed animals, all belonging to her two young children. Her home is packed with kid energy, and you can feel the love she has for her son and daughter within her house. Those kinds of vibes are what we sense with our bodies and will make an impression on us personally and professionally.

Barbara picked up on those vibes. On some level, she perceived there was more to her boyfriend's neglected living space than just the lack of time he claimed. Her body recoiled at the inattention he gave to his home, and, on a gut level, she knew that it symbolized something deeper.

Her boyfriend, on the other hand, admitted to being embarrassed but did not or could not take steps to rectify the situation. Barbara felt instinctively that her boyfriend was expressing a lot through the neglect of his home. Because she was not ready to trust her instinct, she could not admit to herself what his home was telling her. Her body knew the truth, but she ended up overriding its message with her mind.

HOME FRONT

What Barbara experienced was a clear example of how much we pick up information about each other's homes. This does not mean that all carelessly treated living spaces indicate a doomed relationship. No, that is not the case at all. For some, the basic skills of how to set up a home or apartment were never taught. The knowledge that many of us take for granted on how to paint, decorate, or buy furniture can be overwhelming to those who have never had a real home. Not having a home can be defined not only literally but figuratively as well. I've had clients who, growing up, were so emotionally neglected that they cannot imagine settling into a comfortable living space. They unconsciously re-create their past by having just enough material possessions to get by, and only buy the basics. They rarely purchase new items for their homes and will keep using whatever furniture, appliances, or dishware they have until they are broken beyond repair. They grew up having to make do with what they had, never realizing they could have more. Emotional and physical deprivation is what they know, and as we explored in Weeks Three and Four, we often re-create the familiar even if it doesn't serve us any longer.

Rootless

Many people have never had the security of being in one place. Raised in a variety of different environments, they cannot put down roots even as adults. They have either moved frequently or been shuttled between relatives and strangers. These are folks who often do not buy furniture or unpack boxes even if they have been living in a place for a while. It is hard for them to commit to their houses or apartments, because they are unconsciously afraid of having to leave again. Their internal belief is, why bother? Why bother settling into a place when you are bound to move someday? These are people whose bodies are filled with indecision and anxiety when it comes to putting a couch or desk in their living spaces. Their homes become the landscape for all the old fears of being uprooted. What helps is a step-by-step process of identifying what *home* signifies to them.

How about you? Are you aware of what *home* means to you on a body-mind level? Take a look at this checklist and answer the questions to find out.

You don't have to have an answer for everything. Just use the questions to stimulate your imagination and thoughts.

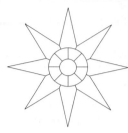

COMPASS POINTS

Home and Heart Checklist

❋ What words or phrases come to mind when you think of the word *home*?

❋ What do you notice in your body when you focus briefly on each of those words?

❋ Name a book you have read that captures your fantasy of the perfect home. How does your body feel when you picture that book?

❋ Name a movie that brings to mind your fantasy of the ideal home. What do you notice in your body when you envision the movie?

❋ What piece of artwork, painting, or magazine cover reflects your idea of home? How does your body feel?

❋ What colors come to mind when you imagine your home being just the way you want it to be?

❋ Is there a piece of music that expresses your feelings about your ideal home? What do you notice in your body when you hear the music?

❋ Is there someone, real or imaginary, whom you identify with the word *home*? How does your body feel when you picture that person?

Imagine where you live now and see if any of the images, words, or sounds you came up with are present in your living space. If not, here is an exercise that will help discover where you may want to be.

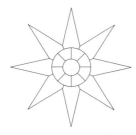

COMPASS POINTS

Exercise: Homeward Bound

1. Close your eyes and focus on how you are breathing.
2. Do the **Four-Part Breathing** exercise.
3. Let your breathing return to normal, but keep your eyes closed.
4. Using your imagination, picture where you would like to live in the world if there were no obstacles. Is it north, south, east, or west?
5. Picture the scenery, feel the air, notice the details of the landscape or buildings.
6. Describe what your home would look like in this place. Be specific with the color, shape, and size.
7. How do you know it is the right place?
8. Where do you feel that sense of knowing in your body?
9. Is it a tactile feeling, an energy feeling, or a visual?
10. Now picture yourself living in that place, walking in the door, sitting in the backyard, looking out the window, or eating in the kitchen.
11. How does your energy or body feel when you imagine yourself there?

12. Now picture a place where you don't like living. (Use your imagination. If nothing comes to mind, picture a dark apartment, a high-rise, or a basement.)

13. How does your energy feel?

14. Now go back to the place you would like to live in.

15. How does your energy feel? Where do you feel that place of knowing?

16. Take deep breaths, in through the nose and out through the mouth, three times.

17. Open your eyes and write down your answers.

HOME AWAY FROM HOME

We all have places we've visited or lived that mattered to us. They could be our childhood homes, cities that inspired us, or villages that offered us rest and restoration. We all have our favorites, and they are as diverse as we are. You can always tell when an environment has had an impact on people. They will describe the place as though it were a delicious meal they had thoroughly enjoyed. The blue sky, tall mountains, ancient streets, and modern buildings are spoken about in reverent tones. The returning travelers' eyes will shine as they convey where they have been, and their whole presence is filled with the happy energy of remembrance. We do reflect outwardly how much we are affected by the location and settings where we spend time.

Places can also inspire change, and for Carol, inspiration was needed. After working very hard for her company, she found herself agonizing over the decision to leave her job. Unacknowledged and overworked, Carol felt trapped in her position. She knew she wanted to leave but was frightened about the unknown. Her mind went back and forth trying to come to some resolution. Fortunately, she had a vacation planned during this time and ended up visiting the Grand Canyon as part of her trip. The experience of seeing the canyon completely changed her perspective on her work situation. Carol went from viewing the world as small and narrow to seeing how spacious it really was. She was able to describe to me the moment she came to a place of peace about her job decision. "I was sitting on a ledge, near the edge of the canyon, looking out at the vast sky and depth of space in front of me. Something in my body just relaxed and opened up, almost as if I was matching the expansiveness I saw unfolding before me. I felt in my body that it was time to leave my job and try something new." Carol came to realize she had more room in her life than she originally thought. She now knew in her heart that she could give notice. A week after she returned, she did just that.

Are there places that have offered you inspiration, restoration, and perspective? Take a moment right now and call up those favorite places in your mind. Notice where and how your body responds to the memory. Is there any place in your life now that can provide the equivalent of what you are remembering? Perhaps a fountain in your city reminds you of that piazza in Italy. Maybe the trees in your local park can soothe you the way a far-off village did in the past. Whenever you need to give your body a break but you can't get away, close your eyes and remember. If at all possible, try to find a little piece of your favorite home away from home where you live today.

HAVEN

Our homes reflect our personalities, history, and emotional life. They reveal much of who we are in regard to where we choose to live and how we care for and decorate our living spaces. Our inner self is reflected through the way we buy or don't buy furniture, the color of our walls, and the objects we choose to display. Each aspect of our home is revealing something about us to ourselves and the world.

I have found that economics can have very little to do with how we inhabit our living spaces. Sure, we may not have a lot financially at different points in our lives, but I have had friends, colleagues, and clients create beautiful homes with very little money. They have either saved up to buy a few special things or they found items that were not expensive but chosen with thoughtfulness. They want to make their homes comfortable, no matter how little money they have.

I have also experienced the opposite: I have known people with lots of money whose houses reflect that sense of neglect and emotional poverty I wrote about earlier. They either purchase many items and let them fall into disarray, or have lots of empty rooms that are filled with dust. This is different from someone who consciously chooses to live in a space with minimal furniture. You can feel the difference between a spare yet clean and flowing home and one that is empty and stark. Whether it's a studio apartment, colonial mansion, or solar-powered ranch, how we inhabit the space we live in is who we are.

Our living spaces also give us messages about what is going on in our external world. If I feel dragged down when I walk into the home I share with my husband, something is off balance. This usually means that too many things have piled up due to the busyness of our lives, and we are feeling overloaded. Usually it turns out to be a blessing in disguise when my body starts reacting to our living space. When I feel uncomfortable, I start to pay attention, rather than cruising along doing tons of activities until I run out of steam. Perhaps you've had the same feeling as well—when your home becomes so cluttered due to your packed schedule that one day you come home and can't find your cat under all the piles? Thank goodness my home has volunteered to let my body know when I've reached my saturation point. There's nothing like some piled up mail and laundry to get you back in touch with yourself. However, sometimes the message needs to get louder.

HOME/LIFE CHANGES

Wendy hated her apartment, a small studio with limited light. Similar to Jason, she felt physically weighed down every time she walked in. The walls were painted a dull white, and even though Wendy was a painter, her apartment did not reflect her artistic nature. She had never bothered to fix it up, and only remained because it was cheap. According to Wendy, living there was only supposed to be temporary. *Temporary* became 15 years, and by the time Wendy and I met she had reached her limit. She felt stuck in her life and unhappy in her home.

Wendy had a strong belief that she could not afford to leave her home and was extremely doubtful about there being other places to move to. Everything felt out of reach. Her body reflected her belief through tension in her lower back and tightness in her upper arms. Wendy shared her financial information with me, and we found it to be solid.

This showed me that she was viewing her living situation through the lens of an old belief. Because she was not ready to give up her view that a new apartment was possible to find, we had to shift our focus. We needed to start with her foundation and make her current apartment more than just a place to exist. We had to make it a home.

Because Wendy could not imagine finding a better place, I needed to appeal to her practical side. I asked her how her ideal home would look or feel if money was no object. Wendy immediately described an apartment overlooking the water with white walls and lots of sunlight. She pictured herself sharing the space with a husband, but not the man she was seeing now. This was revealing because Wendy was as ambivalent about who she was dating as she was about her home. When I had her check in with her body's reaction to her dream home, she said she felt light, happy, and optimistic.

WORKING ON THE FOUNDATION

I asked Wendy if she was willing to capture the essence of her fantasy home and add whatever she could to her current living space. That meant painting the walls, adding plants or colorful hangings—anything that appealed to her artistic side. It was really up to her to make her living space as close, in *feeling*, to her ideal home. Wendy agreed to try. She chose a new wall color, rearranged some furniture, added some colorful carpet, and even bought a decorative water fountain because she loved the sound. These changes totally shifted how her apartment felt to her.

The really fascinating part of this story was that shortly after Wendy fixed up her apartment, she ran into a man whom she had always liked. They started dating, he moved in, and a year and half later they were married. One year after that, they moved to a new apartment that was bigger, sunnier, and yes, close to the water. According to Wendy, the reason these things happened was because fixing up her apartment made her feel good. Because she felt good, she felt more open to the possibilities in her life. Being more open allowed her to meet someone who was a better match for her. Through that romantic partnership, she was able to move and create the home she always dreamed of. This all started with working on Wendy's foundation.

WORKING WITH BELIEFS

When I first met Wendy, she was not ready to give up her core belief about the affordability of another apartment. This was despite the fact that she had money saved up. One way you can tell you have run into a negative core belief either in yourself or with others is when all logic fails to register. There is a resistance, an energetic wall that doesn't budge the perspective. You can state all the facts and statistics you want, but it doesn't make a difference. This is when you have to shift your focus and energy and *work with* the fixed belief as opposed to trying to change it. You have to accept and respect the fact that this particular belief, usually based in fear, needs more time to be dismantled. This does not mean you have to remain stuck. No, it's a matter of pointing your inner compass in a different direction and trying a new route. With Wendy, the journey started within her four walls and then took her right out the front door.

Let us discover whether you have any fixed beliefs about where you live. Remember, a core belief is not something to be ashamed of, it just means that there is usually an emotion attached to it. Some beliefs are positive, and some are negative. Take a look at the following exercise to see if there are any floating around inside.

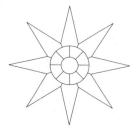

COMPASS POINTS
EXERCISE: HOME BELIEFS

1. Take a deep breath and think about where you live right now.
2. What's the first thing you notice in your body when you picture your home? (You can use any word or description you want—light, expansive, gray fog.)
3. Where do you feel those sensations in your body?
4. When you imagine staying in your home, how does your body feel?
5. When you think about moving somewhere else, what do you notice in your body?
6. Without over-thinking, what beliefs do you have about where you live right now?
   Examples:
   * I'm biding my time.
   * I'm in the right place.
   * I can't leave right now.
   * It's my cave.
7. If you have run into a negative belief about where you live, ask yourself this question: What's one small thing I can do to make my home a better place to live?

8. How does your body feel when you imagine taking that action?

9. When will you take the action?

TIME TO GO

Sometimes we outgrow places that used to be cozy. This could have been your first house, your earliest apartment, or even that room you rented when you left your childhood home. No matter how great it used to be living there, when you are done with it, you know it. Perhaps it is a space you shared with someone you no longer are involved with. Maybe it is because you are through with that particular phase in your life. You have outgrown your former home, and it no longer matches who you are now. I've known friends and clients who have moved from large spaces to small spaces, and vice versa. What seems to matter the most was finding the right fit for who they are now, in their present lives. I believe that when we move willingly from one place to another, we are reflecting the outward manifestation of our internal changes. Moving is a signal from inside that you are headed in a different direction, and your inner voice is what is prompting you to go.

PROFESSIONAL PRESENCE

Besides our home environment, the office or workspace in which we spend time is also chock-full of information. For many, the professional office can be an impersonal and sterile environment. Although it may be hard to carve out space for yourself when you work for others, it's important to try. Finding ways, even small ones, to have your personal identity supported, will help make the hours you put in on the job more tolerable. If you are allowed the latitude to have personal objects or touchstones that make you feel connected to yourself, then do so. Whether you post pictures, artwork, inspiring words, or have a great screen saver, take the time to make the place you spend lots of hours in comfortable. My client Rachel has certain prayers within her sightline to help her get through the stresses of work. This is similar to committing to your living space. If you are not planning to leave your job for a while, make it nice for yourself. Take the time to figure out how you can create the same kind of haven you have at home, in your office environment.

Whether you want to be there or have to be there, creating a comfortable and supportive workspace will help you on the job. Take a moment to review this exercise and see if you are taking care of yourself in your professional environment.

COMPASS POINTS

Exercise: Workplace Beliefs

1. Close your eyes and picture your place of work.

2. Focus on the specific area you work in, whether it's a cubicle or private office.

3. What words come to mind when you envision that place?

4. What do you notice in your body when you imagine yourself sitting in your work place? (Neck feels tight, shoulders feel weighted, chest feels open.)

5. Imagine leaving things exactly how they are. What do you notice in your body? (Energized, blah, stomach tight.)

6. Imagine making one change to your workspace. What would it be?

7. How does your body feel when you imagine that change taking place?

8. What effect would that one change have on the way you feel when you are working?

9. What do you need to do to make this one change happen?

SENDING THE RIGHT SIGNAL

The message you send to others while you are at work will be reflected in your office space. Whether you have four walls or a cubicle, clutter and mess creates the energy of chaos, and others feel it. We are not talking about being perfectly neat all the time, but rather the nonverbal signals you send out about how you operate on the job. I am not the most orderly person when I am writing notes or going through my mail in between clients. But before they come for a session, I make sure my space is organized. I want my clients to feel comfortable and respected for the personal work they undertake in my office. I take the time to make sure the room they enter is welcoming.

If you do work for yourself, you have the opportunity to create a workspace that reflects many of the core values you chose in Week Two. Your personal style is unique to you, and how you manage your professional space will affect your success. How so? By creating quality, unspoken, visual statements that your current and potential clients will pick up on. These range from the furniture you choose for them to sit on, to the art on the walls to the reading material you have on display and the cleanliness of your bathrooms. Of course there are some things you may not be able to control, such as the outside of the building or the color of the lobby. But how your clients and business colleagues feel once they enter your space is directly in your hands. You need to decide what professional impression you want to give others when they enter your workplace. If you need help with this, go back to the **Core Values** list you created in Week Two and see if any of them are showing up in your workspace.

COMPASS POINTS

EXERCISE: PROFESSIONAL IMPRESSIONS

1. What professional impressions do you want others to take away when they work with you? (What words or phrases come to mind?)

   Examples:

   ❀   Competent.

   ❀   Warm, caring.

   ❀   Professional; I get the job done.

2. Now close your eyes and picture your office.

3. What words come to mind when you envision your space? (Clean, elegant, shabby, cozy.)

4. What do you notice in your body when you imagine yourself sitting in your workspace? (Relaxed, body feels upright, chest feels tight.)

5. Does what you feel in your body match the professional message you want others to get about you?

6. If not, what's one step you can take this week to get your workplace in alignment with the professional impression you want to create?

ENTRANCES

When you decide to commit to a professional space, it can stir up unexpected feelings. That's how it was for Tom, a massage therapist. Throughout the years, Tom's healing touch and kindness had created a following of loyal clients. But he had always rented office space, on an hourly basis from others, to do his massages. Though Tom was doing fairly well, he knew he could take his practice further by getting an office of his own. When we discussed him finding his own space, it brought up quite a bit of fear. With exploration, he was able to pinpoint two specific ones: the fear of failing and the fear of being a more powerful person in the world.

I asked Tom to imagine himself in his own office and to picture all the details he wanted in the space. After he had the image, I told him to check in with his body and observe its reaction. The first thing he noticed was a fluttering in his stomach that traveled up to his chest. When he checked in his body on what the sensation was expressing, he said "You know, when I first focused on it, I thought it was the same old fear, but it's actually excitement." He then laughed and said, "I'm a little nervous about being excited, but I think I can get over it." I asked how his body knew he could get over his nervousness, and he said, "I'm an information guy. I know inside that if I take it step by step and get the information I need to rent an office, I will feel calmer. That's what I need to do." And six months later he did. He now works out of his own office and is thriving.

Tom's experience shows us that moving toward a dream is an ongoing process of which we can be in charge. The choices we make do not have to be immediate, nor black or white. The choices do not have to be either taking the plunge or staying exactly where we are. They are about the little steps in between that keep leading us toward where we need to go. One step informs the next, and so on. Such was the case with my friend Rochelle.

EXITS

Rochelle, a successful and dynamic movement specialist, had longed to have her own studio to work with her individual clients and teach a variety of fitness classes. She was able to find a space in her neighborhood that fit the bill, and poured her heart into creating a warm and welcoming environment. Pretty soon her studio was filled with a range of classes and workshops. Rochelle felt successful and content. She had fulfilled a fantasy she had imagined for a long time. What a shock it was to her when that dream began to change.

In time, Rochelle's movement studio began to feel like a weight to her, not because of the work she was doing with her clients, but because of the work she was doing on herself. Always a person who valued introspection, Rochelle had spent the past few years doing her own personal healing. She used the time to weed out anything in her personal life that kept her from being happy. Her inner voice began to emerge. What she discovered was that she wanted to be a teacher and speaker. She wanted to share the work she was currently doing, but in a different form. Her studio space no longer fit her. Similar to Tom, once she clarified and accepted the message, she emotionally and practically prepared to leave the studio she had created. When she was ready to go, which was a year-long process, she closed her space and began her new career.

In this chapter we looked at how spaces and places affect us. It's vital to have your home and office support your spirit and reflect who you are. Use any or all of the exercises in this chapter to help you figure how to make wherever you are a haven.

COMPASS POINTS
WEEK SIX ASSIGNMENTS

1. Use the **Four-Part Breathing** exercise whenever you need to regain your focus.

2. Continue with the **What Does My Body Need?** exercise and use it any time you need to figure out a decision.

3. Bring something into your current home that captures the essence of your core values from Week Three and matches your personality. It could be as small as a picture, or as dramatic as a new piece of furniture. Be sure that, whatever you bring, you put it in a prominent place so you can't miss it. See if you notice how it affects your energy when you are there.

4. If you are not living where you want to live,
    complete the **Homeward Bound** exercise from this
    chapter on a daily basis. At the end of the week,
    review your answers and notice what shows up
    consistently. If relocating is difficult at this time, how
    can you create more of where you want to live in
    your current home?

5. If you are looking to upgrade your professional
    impression at your job or in your own business, go
    over the **Workplace Beliefs** exercise in this chapter
    and do the **Professional Impressions** exercise on a
    daily basis. Read over your answers at the end of the
    week and see what steps you are being prompted to
    take by your inner voice.

PART II:
Your Journey Continues

(((((((((Chapter Eight)))))))))

Your Inner Voice Journey

We never know how high we are / Till we are called to rise;
/ And then, if we are true to plan, / Our statures touch the skies.
—Emily Dickinson

This book has been about using your instinct and intuition through the body-mind connection. In this final chapter, I wanted to talk about the journey of personal growth, and what you can encounter as you continue forward. Though this book has included a 6-week program, many of you will continue to evolve and expand throughout a lifetime. No matter what areas of spiritual or personal expansion you explore, your inner voice is yours to rely on.

PERSONAL GROWTH

I had the pleasure of attending my friend Amy's graduation from a three-year program of spiritual study. In addition

to her work as a therapist, she had decided to become an
ordained interfaith minister. I've known Amy for quite a
while, and she has always cultivated her spirit in a variety of
unique ways. Whether she has studied meditation or Sufism
or taught classes in A Course in Miracles, Amy's soul has
thirsted for spiritual knowledge. But I was surprised to find
that this wasn't always the case. In fact, as she shared with
me, her journey of personal growth started in an unusual way.

"About 15 years ago, I was watching television and a
program came on about military training that showed what
the newly enlisted went through to become soldiers. One
thing that jumped out was that boot camp was about six
weeks long. During that time, the recruits were conditioned
mentally and physically to conform to the military's code
of behavior." What intrigued Amy was the fact that all the
participants came from different backgrounds. Yet that
didn't seem to influence the outcome at all—in fact, most
everybody adapted. What did seem to matter was the commitment the newcomers brought to the training process.
They were open and willing to try, which allowed them to
give over to the rigorous experience. (By the way, I know
my program is six weeks long, but I swear I never saw the
show!)

Amy's television show got her thinking. If the military
could bring about behavior modification in six weeks, then
perhaps she, in a similarly finite period of time, could change
some aspects of her own life. There was something about
having a commitment and specific time frame that appealed
to her. She felt it would give her something by which to
measure her success, and began to search for the right course
of study. As often happens with inner journeys, a book that
fit her needs showed up.

The book that caught Amy's attention was on how to change one's attitude in order to achieve business success. The book basically asked readers to look at their life experiences from a glass-half-full perspective instead of glass-half-empty; to make the effort and reframe how life could be approached on a day-to-day basis. The book promised a shift in the reader's general outlook if the techniques were applied in a consistent manner. Amy committed to the challenge of the author and found that it worked. Through the magic of television, Amy's spiritual journey began. Fifteen years later, she was a minister.

A CALL FROM WITHIN

The path we choose for personal growth is either an experience we consciously choose or one that happens to us. More than any other area of our lives, when we are feeling a personal emptiness, our inner voice gets called into action. Whether we undertake the quest willingly or struggle against it, the impetus for change makes itself known. Amy's catalyst was a television program, but it wouldn't have had an effect if she wasn't already searching. Some people describe their growth as a thunderbolt of awakening, and others speak of slowly emerging from a private fog. Many people talk of receiving messages from out of the blue or having special moments that changed their lives, such as hearing God's voice, hitting rock bottom with an addiction, or experiencing an amazing recovery from illness.

There are others who fight against personal growth until the bitter end. They engage in self-destructive behavior and appear not to be interested in another way of living. They turn from their inner voice and find outside means to quiet their pain. This sometimes results in self-medication or addictions to substances (illegal or legal). They endure daily chaos and pain, because they do not believe there is another way. Not until things get so bad and life is intolerable do they finally listen and accept the call from within.

Most people battling addictions are not enjoying the ongoing method they have picked to numb themselves. They are trying to manage a great deal of emotional pain and have chosen something that gives them immediate relief. They've found a destructive way to cope with self-defeating thoughts and feelings that have not been resolved. This doesn't mean, if you are on the receiving end of someone's destructive behavior, that you should accept it. That would be harmful to you. It's about understanding how out of control the addicted person feels, and for you to find ways to care for yourself while he or she is struggling. Using the **What Does My Body Need?** exercise from Week One is good way to reinforce self-care.

How we get to the place where our soul cries out for expansion is our tale to tell. What we ultimately choose to explore is about using our inner voice. Finding the true connection between body and mind is what keeps our spirit alive and guides us toward the personal development we are seeking. What's *your* body telling you about your need for growth?

Messages and Messengers

Why we turn to one form of soul-searching as opposed to another is unique to each of us. We may notice a sense of emptiness and dissatisfaction inside that no activity or "thing" can fill. There might be a feeling that we need more: more knowledge, more inspiration, more understanding of who we are and what our purpose is. This could be the very reason you picked up this book. Something clicked with you when you saw the title or read what it offers. Like Amy, we can find the message or messenger in any medium.

When you decide to explore who you are, there is vulnerability and uncertainty. There are deep questions to answer and many sources in which to find those answers. I've had clients who were drawn to formal religion, 12-step programs, spiritual groups, and individual meditation. I've known others who went back to school, found a therapist, changed their eating habits, and started exercising. The range of choices is as varied as the people who choose them. That is the great thing about personal growth: it is truly personal.

When you decide to expand your spirit and explore your life, you end up taking a leap of faith. Because the call from within is usually a *feeling* more than a thought, this is where your body's compass will assist you. How your body responds will be the best guide to helping you figure out whether what you have chosen is helpful or harmful. Maybe it's surprising to think that personal growth can be harmful, but it can be when the concepts of discipline and rigidity are confused.

LOOKING OUTWARD

Jenny was down in the dumps about her work situation and finances. A former corporate executive, she had lost her last job due to the company's downsizing. She found herself unsure about what steps to take, and while she was contemplating what to do she ran into a friend. Jenny's friend told her about a group she was involved with that offered great personal transformation. The group promised those who joined that they would learn to release hidden fears and habits by learning the organization's methodology. The program seemed to offer a lot of what Jenny was looking for: support from others and a straightforward plan for approaching life. She decided to attend an open house and later described to me her initial impressions.

"I was a bit scared when I arrived, and while most people seemed friendly, there was also another feeling in the room, almost an air of competitiveness. Everyone was upbeat but I felt this weird pressure from the members as if they really wanted me to know how happy they were." Now, Jenny wasn't against folks being upbeat, and she was open to feeling positive, but she found the participants' energy overwhelming. They seemed to be talking *at* her, expounding on their achievements as opposed to finding out about who she was.

Later in the evening, there was a lecture in which the organization's programs were discussed. The presenter was forceful and dynamic in his talk. He called upon many people in the audience and asked them to share how much their lives had changed by using the group's methods. At the end of the night, the speaker told the audience that if they left without signing up for a class, it was a sure sign they were resistant to change.

Jenny felt scared, because without knowing much about her, she had been typed as fearful person due to her hesitancy about joining. She knew she needed to make shifts in her life, and because she was feeling so vulnerable, she decided to sign up for a class. Two years later, Jenny came to see me. She hadn't found a secure job, had spent thousands of dollars on classes, and was still feeling insecure. What happened to the promise of transformation?

MIND WITHOUT HEART

If we try to make changes with just our minds but do not include our bodies in the process, we can only shift so far. No matter what the system, if there are unresolved emotional issues within us, they will make themselves known when we try to expand our spirit. Those are the deeply rooted parts of our personality that cannot be talked over or bypassed simply by absorbing a new way of thinking. I've known people who, because of their spiritual practice, chanted in meditation for hours, yet neglected their families. Others praised a particular method of personal growth, but could not control their compulsive behavior. And some, like Jenny, paid money for classes or guidance and ended up close to bankruptcy.

When there is an obvious difference between your day-to-day functioning and the time you are spending learning a new methodology, it's an indication that the mind-body conversation is not happening. The dialog between the body and mind that gives you important information is either overwhelmed or being held at bay. When that occurs, there is a tendency to miss and ignore the signals from your inner compass. This causes your perspective to be out of balance, because, if you are placing your attention outside of yourself, trying to please someone or some group's ideals, you don't have much time for your own insight.

In order to make sure that what has been promised to happen is actually happening, you need to keep checking in with your instinct. Take the time daily to consult with your body and see if it is offering an opinion. You want to make sure you are in sync with *you*. If you are feeling anxious and out of control in your day-to-day life, but are being reproached for not committing more to your practice or program, something needs a second look.

CHASTISING VS. CHALLENGING

There is a difference between being chastised for your efforts and being challenged. When you decide to look inward, you will run into both. If you are chastised for not doing *enough* in your quest for personal growth, there is an implicit message of judgment. This has a restrictive feel to it and causes you to second-guess your natural responses. Being challenged, on the other hand, does not include criticism—though to be honest it initially can feel just as bad. I had my own significant experience of being challenged when I was trying to grow as a therapist.

During the course of my five-year training program, we were required to participate in a group to process the feelings and thoughts that came up during school. At one point I was challenged by my classmates for not being more emotionally open with them. I was furious and hurt that they viewed me that way, and I wanted to withdraw from the group. But the school's leader helped me realize that my colleagues were pushing me, because they wanted more for and from me, as opposed to wanting me to feel "less than." Though it was tough, it ultimately showed me a way to be more connected to others. I felt the caring of the group even as they asked me to grow.

DISCIPLINE

Others have had the experience of being challenged when they chose a school of spiritual study or 12-step program. After the initial relief of joining a group of likeminded people and perhaps putting down a self-destructive activity, they run into the struggle of what's required to face themselves. Whether it's the 12 steps, the discipline of meditation, or learning how to listen, they are challenged to look at their past behavior. The dismantling of long-held beliefs can be humbling, but that struggle becomes part of the journey toward inner awareness.

The key distinction between being challenged and being chastised is how you feel after you understand the encounter. It's the difference between feeling inadequate and empowered. If you are receiving pressure to become more involved in a group or to spend more money on additional classes, and are being judged for hesitating, it's time to examine your choice. If you are being challenged to face your fears but are treated with compassion, you will have the opportunity to blossom. Using your body's inner signals will help you perceive the difference.

FINAL AUTHORITY

Besides the career and financial issues in her life, Jenny had a history of not asserting her needs. This kept her from speaking up professionally, as well as in most of her personal relationships. Those unresolved emotional issues made her susceptible to a community that promised her a different life but also pressured her to do more with the group. Jenny was out of touch with her inner voice and her own authority. The whole time she was involved with the group mentioned, she had a constant feeling of unease in her body.

If you are questioning the choice you have made, use your body-mind connection to help you figure out the answer. The question to ask is, "Is my life getting better?" While you are learning, expanding, and studying, is your life getting better? Pay attention to how your body responds, as it will help you track the aspects of your life that are moving forward. You then become the final authority on what is or is not working for you.

BLACK AND WHITE

Trusting your body compass will help you master the complexity of personal growth. At the beginning of your journey, you may find yourself sticking closely to the guidelines of whatever program or course of study you have chosen. Being on a structured path is a fine way to learn and discover things about yourself. Once you have determined it is the right place for you, you will begin to notice that one size does not fit all. There will be aspects that you love and parts that don't fit you. If that's the case, try not to think in terms of black and white, or right and wrong. Ask questions of the mentors you trust, and continue to refine your own belief system. Like Amy, who has created a spiritual practice from the different methods she has studied, you too will find ways that are uniquely yours. For additional support and insight, you can run your perceptions by any of the people you listed on your support list from Week Four.

WALKING THE TALK

In life, you will have people guide you for various reasons at different times. Some you'll be drawn to, and others you'll meet by chance. Each one will serve a purpose and help you along at a particular point of your journey. As you learn from them, you will incorporate into your belief systems what they offer that is meaningful to you. Some mentors remain with you throughout your life, and others you will leave. Either way, the positive influence they have upon you will remain.

One of the best ways to gauge whether a mentor or leader is right for you is to notice if he is "walking the talk." Is he modeling his beliefs in thought, word, and deed to the best of his ability? You want to have the sense that the person advising you is living by the principles he is encouraging you to explore. Is she caring, compassionate, and stable in her own life? These are important issues to think about when you are searching for guidance. You want to have an inner sense of security when you allow someone to mentor you personally and spiritually. How do figure that out? Use your body to confirm your perceptions. Choose the right mentor at the right time by reminding yourself of how you felt with people from your past who had a positive impact on you.

When you go back in time, you will probably recall certain teachers, coaches, or religious leaders who influenced you in a beneficial way. Think of all the different activities, classes, and sports you participated in when you were growing up. A wide range of people probably crossed your path during those years. And of those individuals, a handful of them, I'm sure, will stand out. Many of them supported you, challenged you, or were even tough on you. When you focus on them, you can probably remember and describe the reasons they had an effect on you. Connecting to *how* and *why* they made an impression is a great guide for choosing mentors in the future. Look at the following checklist to help you remember your "teachers" of the past.

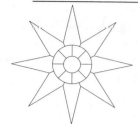

COMPASS POINTS

PEOPLE OF INFLUENCE CHECKLIST

❀ Take a moment and think of the people in your life who had an impact on you growing up.

❀ Who were those people? (Teacher, coach, therapist, instructor.)

❀ What qualities did they have that made you remember them? (Warm, caring, smart.)

❀ What do you feel in your body as you recall those qualities? (Calm, motivated, a spring your step.)

❀ Why were those qualities important to you?

❀ Do you feel you need those qualities in your life today?

❀ How can you provide yourself with that kind of support?

❀ Where or to whom can you go to receive it?

❀ When you imagine receiving it, how does your body feel?

UNEXPECTED BARRIERS

When you are looking for transformation, there is a feeling of relief when you take action and feel the effect. There is a positive feeling and sense of hope that your life will become better. Those are the fundamental aspects to look for when you are exploring personal growth. Are the areas of your life that were stagnant and unfulfilling starting to shift? Do you feel more connected to who you are and what you want for yourself? As you start to examine how your personal journey is going, these questions will emerge and need to be answered. You also may find some surprising and unexpected roadblocks as you start to grow.

Robert always had a love of drawing and photography, but, throughout the years, he had lost touch with that side of himself. A bright, funny, and spiritually aware man, he had put aside his creative interests in order to work and raise a family. When we met, he was feeling a sense of emptiness in his life. His children were grown, and his relationship with his wife was stable, but who he was as an individual was not being satisfied. After exploring what he felt was lacking in his life, Robert remembered how much he enjoyed taking pictures and sketching. He felt happy to reconnect to that part of himself that had been buried for so long. He decided to buy a camera and purchase some drawing pencils. What a shock it was for him, then, when his fear decided to pay a visit.

CLEANING OUT THE GUTTERS

When Robert made the decision to buy art supplies, he was surprised by the sudden emergence of negative feelings. Old judgments surfaced about his right to be creative, and he found himself paralyzed. He complained to me that he couldn't understand what was stopping him. All he had to do was go to the store and buy drawing pencils, but he couldn't seem to. What appeared to be an easy task for anyone else actually brought Robert face to face with some old insecurity. What was the insecurity? After all these years, he was finally going to put his creative needs first. Not his children's, not his wife's, but his. And that was a big deal to

Robert. There was no one else to focus on except him, and it was unfamiliar territory.

When I asked Robert to check with his body to see what it had to say about buying art supplies, he said his stomach felt jumpy. As he focused on the jumpy feeling, Robert told me he was surprised. Instead of the sensation being only fear, he realized there was a lot of "let's do it" energy mixed in. In fact, there was much less fear than he realized. His instinct was saying *go for it and let it happen!* Once he connected to his body and understood its reaction, he was able to get a clear sense of what he was feeling. And the signal was "Go."

Robert discovered that the negative thoughts he was having were actually just on the surface, not what he felt deep down. He realized that his initial reactions and negative thoughts were an old habit that kept him from taking action. Like the leaves that clog the gutters on a house, his old beliefs initially kept him from asserting more of his creative needs. Even though Robert's intent to grow was sincere, the flow of his creativity had gotten stuck. The negative beliefs needed to be cleaned out, and by listening to his body's truth he was able to get a more accurate picture of how to move ahead. By focusing on his stomach and taking it step by step, Robert realized he could take time for his own needs in addition to the needs of others. He also knew he didn't have to be an accomplished artist immediately; he could simply take pleasure in drawing to get started.

As change starts to happen, you too may find yourself facing some of the reasons you have been held back. When you take the actions you need in order to grow, deep feelings may show up that seem contradictory to what you are trying to accomplish. Try not to judge yourself for feeling scared, angry, or even sad. Those emotions can be our greatest teachers, and it's important to understand why they are showing up.

UNPOPULAR EMOTIONS

There is a fallacy that occurs in personal growth that has to do with emotional expression. The idea seems to be that if you feel what I call "unpopular emotions," you will attract negative things into your life. Unpopular emotions are feelings such as anger, grief, fear, sadness, terror, and despair. These responses are sometimes judged, because they don't fall into the "positive feeling" camp. Yet, these and all our emotions belong to the palette of human expression and make up who we are. As the therapist Carl Jung once said, "Even a happy life cannot be without a measure of darkness, and the word *happy* would lose its meaning if it were not balanced by sadness. It is far better to take things as they come along with patience and equanimity."

His last line is the one I feel is so important to hear in regard to painful feelings. Don't fall into the trap of thinking or believing that emotions that are not 100 percent positive will create negativity in your life. We need the patience and acceptance to feel what we need to, without being afraid that we will create bad circumstances for ourselves. My experience has shown that there is an inevitable shift in energy and attitude when you give yourself the permission to feel what you need to. That acceptance strengthens the bond between heart and head, and moves you to a place of self-trust. Then you'll know and understand what your next steps should be.

WHEN STUCK MEANS STUCK

There may be times when you find yourself with a negative mindset that just won't shift. This is different from unpopular emotions, and is about chronic negative beliefs that are formed early on in life. When a pattern of thinking is chronic, it has been going on for a while and does not seem to be changing. This type of thinking kicks in automatically, and when it does, people find it hard to get out of their own way. Remember Wendy and her apartment belief in Week Six? That's the attitude I'm referring to, and it develops through time. Along the way you start to believe that it is the truth instead of a distortion.

If you find yourself in this pattern of thinking, it's usually due to a psychological or emotional reason that may be eluding you. This is one of the key signs that a split has formed between your body and mind. Berating yourself for not being able to shift your view will only make it worse, and lowers your self-esteem. Imagine yelling at someone who is afraid and unable to do something he doesn't know how to do yet. You probably can't picture doing so, but it's how many people speak to themselves when they get stuck. Most people don't find it motivating, and it is actually quite cruel when you think of it. Instead, shift the language of blame and instead give yourself the gift of support. Use the **Achievement Validation Checklist** from Week One to get you started. If things still feel difficult, find a good therapist or counselor to help you discover and work through the source of your negative beliefs.

FALSE, YET FAMILIAR, SECURITY BLANKETS

You probably have heard the expression, "Two steps forward, one step back." I think it's the perfect phrase for what you can expect with personal growth. As you evolve spiritually and emotionally, it's inevitable that you will want to return to familiar ways that you know so well. Back to those old, not-so-productive ways of behaving that used to feel good. The longing to do so can throw you off-course if you don't take the time to understand why it is happening.

I have worked with people who, after months or even years of self-growth, found themselves reverting back to behaviors that weren't physically or mentally good for them. This might have been calling an old boyfriend or girlfriend who wasn't so nice. They may have dipped back into a former self-destructive pattern of eating, drinking, or substance use. The negative and distorted thinking that Robert experienced when he explored his creativity is similar to this view others had of themselves. The most interesting part was that this "backtracking" often happened when the person was going through a period of great personal expansion. My clients found it mind-boggling and were thrown by their desire to retreat from the good things they were creating in their lives. They would ask me why they would want to turn to something that would impede their progress. My answer was, and is: change, no matter how much we want it, invites both excitement and fear. The excitement is wonderful and exhilarating. The fear? Unexpected.

There is a vulnerability and anxiety that occurs with change. When we transform who we are, we step out of our comfort zone and stretch in ways we have longed for. You would think that achieving what we have dreamt about would cause happiness. It does. But it also shifts the emotional landscape of who we are. We feel the loss of our identity, the one we know so well. This is often when we want to turn to false, yet familiar, security blankets such as those old relationships and behaviors that defined who we were before change occurred. We "knew" ourselves with that person from our past or while doing those destructive activities. Now, when we think of turning to those old ways, it's because we imagine they will provide comfort, but it's a false way to manage the anxiety of the new. What you really need is a way to catch up to the new you.

The next time you find yourself wanting to turn to an old pattern of behavior, take a few moments to check in with your body and see if it can help you figure out what you are looking for. Try this exercise to see if the choice you are leaning toward is actually right for you.

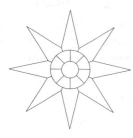

COMPASS POINTS

Exercise: Catch Up to the New You

1. Close your eyes and focus on your breathing.
2. Make a conscious effort to inhale deeply through your nose, expanding your chest, stomach, and abdomen. Exhale slowly through your mouth. Do this three or four times. Let your breathing return to normal.
3. As you sit with you eyes closed, imagine yourself returning to the old ways of behaving.
4. Notice how your body feels when you picture the person or activity from the past.
5. Ask yourself these questions:

❀ Does the **fantasy** of what it will be like to return to the old way of being match the **reality** of what it will give me?

❀ Will I **get** what I want or am I just **hoping to get** what I want?

❀ What is it that I am really looking for to support my personal growth? (Comfort, reassurance, encouragement, information.)

❀ What does my body feel about the answers?

❀ Which sources or people will provide me with the love, help, or inspiration to keep me moving forward?

❀ How does my body feel when I imagine receiving that support?

❀ Who can I reach out to this week?

❀ What opinion does my body have about my choice?

6. Take a deep breath and open your eyes. Write down your answers in your notebook.

Once you identify what you need, see if you can reach out and provide for yourself the healthy support you are seeking. This is another great time to use the support system list you created in Week Four of the individuals who are in your corner. After all, there is nothing wrong with wanting or needing a security blanket. You just want to make sure the material is of good quality.

If, down the road, you find yourself overwhelmed with negative thinking and fear, use the following exercise to help move you from that place. It will help you shift your perspective and give your body a chance to voice an alternative opinion.

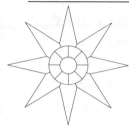

COMPASS POINTS

Exercise: When Fear Comes Calling

1. Close your eyes and sit quietly. Slowly inhale and exhale five times. (If you are experiencing a lot of mind chatter, use the **Four-Part Breathing** exercise.)

2. Focus on any area in your body that feels stuck or tight. Try to breathe into that part of your body.

3. Let your breathing return to normal.

4. Ask yourself what you are feeling. If specific words don't come to mind, then describe the part of your body that is feeling stuck any way you want.

   For example: My shoulders are bound like wire.

   My jaw feels like a rusty hinge.

   My neck feels rubbery.

5. If you are feeling upset when you do this exercise, ask yourself, without judgment, what you need in order to release those feelings.

   ❀ Do you need to reach out to someone? (Friend, therapist, significant other.)

   ❀ Do you need to do something physical? (Walk, dance, run, stretch.)

   ❀ Do you need to watch a movie that touches your heart?

   ❀ Do you need to listen to music that inspires you or makes you cry?

6. Tell yourself that you have the capacity to feel a range of emotions, and each one is valid.

7. Open your eyes.

When you gently remind yourself that emotions are neither good nor bad, you give yourself the permission to be human and imperfect. As you affirm your right to feel what you need to, you will heal and become more whole as a person. I have included some final exercises for you this week to help you continue onward.

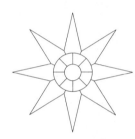

COMPASS POINTS
BONUS ASSIGNMENTS

1. Continue with **Four-Part Breathing** exercise and the **What Does My Body Need?** exercise any time you need to make a decision in your life.

2. Do the **Catch Up to the New You** exercise two days this week.

3. For one week, write down, on a daily basis, all the ways you notice your life is changing. Share at least two changes with someone you trust.

(((((((((Conclusion)))))))))

All you need in order to allow your inner voice to emerge is the willingness to try. Whether it is a journey for the future or one that has started in the past six weeks, bringing your awareness to power the body-mind connection is the first step. When you open to the idea that the body and mind do work together, you invite possibility into your life.

Whether you have done one, five, or all of the exercises in this book, you have opened the door to the idea of change. You can create the relationships, career, home, and spiritual life you want by trusting the wise part of you that knows the truth. That knowledge brings a sense of self-acceptance and hope, which is the turning point in any personal journey.

As you accept who you are and the truth of what you feel, you become more empowered in the world. You no longer have to jump back and forth between your heart and

head, because they will be in harmony. The choices and decisions you make going forward will be based on what feels
right for you. Your instinct and intuition will become familiar friends, ones that you can access when you need to.
If you do lose your way, you can always return to what you
have written and shared with yourself while reading this
book. Take the time to do so and you will remember how
wise your inner voice can be. You will be reminded of who
you are and in what direction your body compass is pointing you. When you get into your body, you get into your
life. When you get into your life, you are truly living.

—Karol Ward

(((((((((INDEX)))))))))

(((((((((ABOUT THE AUTHOR)))))))))

Karol Ward, LCSW, is a licensed psychotherapist, nationally recognized speaker, and writer. She bases her work in the fields of communication and personal development on the importance of the body-mind connection. Karol teaches people how to use their bodies as a compass for decision-making. She shows others how to access, notice, and apply the information that a strong body-mind connection can offer for success. This knowledge is then used for better communication and decision-making, and to create goals in all areas of life.

Ward holds an MA in social work from Fordham University, certification from The Center for Reichian Energetic Therapy, and is certified as a Level 11 EMDR practitioner. Karol is a member of the National Association of Social Workers, the New York State Society for Clinical Social Work, and New

York Women in Communication. She combines her training as a psychotherapist with her passion for communication by conducting a variety of presentations and workshops for such clients as Viacom/MTV, The 92nd Street Y-Makor-Steinhardt Center, The Renfrew Center Foundation, Integrative Healthcare Symposium, IDEA Health and Fitness Association, Hunter College, Polycystic Ovarian Syndrome Association, Fashion Institute of Technology, Professional Women's Alliance, McBurney YMCA, In Fitness & In Health, National Association of Women Business Owners, and Dowling College.

With a degree in Psychology and Communication, Karol understands how information is perceived. She coaches and teaches individuals how to effectively communicate to a variety of audiences for maximum impact. Appearances include QPTV, WOR 710HD, WARL 1320AM, WBNW 1120AM, WPLM 1390AM, TalkZone Radio, HotRadio125, WNLK 1350AM, the *Lisa Birnbach Radio Show*, and Mosa Radio Network. Karol is a regular contributor to the Websites DivineCaroline and Integrative Practitioners. She has been featured on MSNBC.com, AOL.com, and written for, and contributed as an expert to, *Cosmo, CosmoGirl!, Experience Life Magazine, IDEA Fitness Journal, Essence Magazine,* and *Best Body Magazine.* For more information or to book Karol as a speaker, contact her at *www.karolward.com.*

lonely planet

California

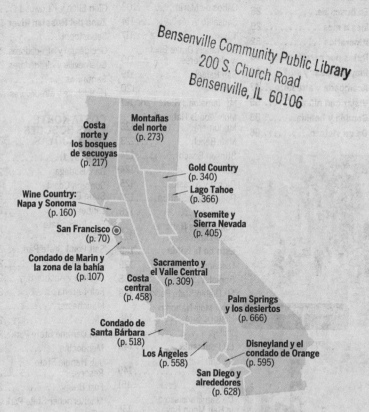

EDICIÓN ESCRITA Y DOCUMENTADA POR

Sara Benson,

Andrew Bender, Alison Bing, Celeste Brash, Tienlon Ho, Beth

Kohn, Adam Skolnick, John A. Vlahides

BARRY WINIKER / GETTY IMAGES ©

VENICE BOARDWALK P. 569

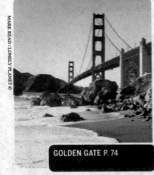

MARK READ / LONELY PLANET ©

GOLDEN GATE P. 74